Putting Truth in Its
Place

A Journey to Intimacy with God

DAWN WALDA AND CO-WRITER JULIA WALDA

WESTBOW
PRESS®
A DIVISION OF THOMAS NELSON
& ZONDERVAN

Copyright © 2021 Dawn Walda and Co-writer Julia Walda.

All rights reserved. No part of this book may be used or reproduced by any means, graphic, electronic, or mechanical, including photocopying, recording, taping or by any information storage retrieval system without the written permission of the author except in the case of brief quotations embodied in critical articles and reviews.

This book is a work of non-fiction. Unless otherwise noted, the author and the publisher make no explicit guarantees as to the accuracy of the information contained in this book and in some cases, names of people and places have been altered to protect their privacy.

WestBow Press books may be ordered through booksellers or by contacting:

WestBow Press
A Division of Thomas Nelson & Zondervan
1663 Liberty Drive
Bloomington, IN 47403
www.westbowpress.com
844-714-3454

Because of the dynamic nature of the Internet, any web addresses or links contained in this book may have changed since publication and may no longer be valid. The views expressed in this work are solely those of the author and do not necessarily reflect the views of the publisher, and the publisher hereby disclaims any responsibility for them.

Any people depicted in stock imagery provided by Getty Images are models, and such images are being used for illustrative purposes only.
Certain stock imagery © Getty Images.

Scripture quotations marked NLT are taken from the Holy Bible, New Living Translation, Copyright © 1996, 2004, 2015 by Tyndale House Foundation. Used by permission of Tyndale House Publishers, Inc., Carol Stream, Illinois 60188. All rights reserved.

Scripture quotations marked NIV are taken from The Holy Bible, New International Version®, NIV® Copyright © 1973, 1978, 1984, 2011 by Biblica, Inc.® Used by permission. All rights reserved worldwide.

Scripture quotations marked ESV taken from The Holy Bible, English Standard Version® (ESV®), Copyright © 2001 by Crossway, a publishing ministry of Good News Publishers. All rights reserved.

Scripture quotations marked GNT are taken from the Good News Translation® (Today's English Version, Second Edition). Copyright © 1992 American Bible Society. All rights reserved.

Scripture quotations marked ASV are taken from the American Standard Bible.

Interior Image Credit: Michaela Walda

ISBN: 978-1-6642-2943-3 (sc)
ISBN: 978-1-6642-2944-0 (hc)
ISBN: 978-1-6642-2942-6 (e)

Library of Congress Control Number: 2021906640

Print information available on the last page.

WestBow Press rev. date: 04/07/2021

When I think of the word *dedication*, I am struck by the ideals of its twins, *commitment* and *partnership*. Their united front offers and gives strength to that which has been given to. And so it's here that I am giving a shout out of thanks to those who have been committed in partnership with this book writing task. I cannot articulate in detail each of your contributions, but know that as you are listed, I am tearfully giving thanks for your unending love, support, care, and encouragement you have so faithfully offered. So, in no particular order I present to you my cheering squad:
John, Jacob, Courtney and Michaela, Alex,
Trish, Eilish, Steve, and Ellen.
And my beloved,
Jesus.

Disclaimer

I do not claim to possess a recognised authorisation to speak to the whole subject of mental health. For its subject is vast, complex, and requires much learning and understanding. Its field of study is beyond that which I have experienced, but I have been privy to my own personal journey in and through mental health as well as family and friend's experiences.

I do not profess that I am qualified in any way to speak about any medical means for treatment of mental health disorders or diseases.

So, in lieu of all things discussed, projected, and declared within the pages of this book, I will limit my context of the term "mental health" to be that which is seen, experienced, and understood through one's mind, the mind being that which is seen as "involving behaviours, thinking and mood. In general, mental illness a condition that impairs a person's ability to think, feel, process, and respond to life's situations" (www.gotquestions.org) in ways that are deemed as normal and healthy. The term "health" being defined simply as "the state of being free from illness" (dictionary.com).

Contents

Chapter 1	Let Us Introduce Ourselves	1
Chapter 2	Introduction to the Renewing of the Mind	9
Chapter 3	First Things First: Love	15
Chapter 4	Intimacy with God	23
Chapter 5	Intimacy with God: The Practical Application	35
Chapter 6	"I Am Who You Say I Am"	43
Chapter 7	Who Do You Say I Am?	53
Chapter 8	Being Intentional: Being Deliberate and Purposed within Your Intentions	61
Chapter 9	Repentance	71
Chapter 10	Change	79
Chapter 11	Challenge Accepted?	87

One

Let Us Introduce Ourselves

Together, Julia and I want to invite you into our journey. To a place of sweet intimacy. Beginning at my kitchen table over a hot cup of tea.

Dawn Walda

Welcome! I'm so excited for you to join us on our first book adventure. My daughter-in-law and I have been on a rather exciting journey of preparing these thoughts, experiences, and truths for you, our readers. Neither one of us have written a book before, and truth be told, we both thought the whole concept was just scary and, well, incredibly daunting. I thought my thoughts and experiences were just that: mine. No one really needed or wanted to read them; that was until the onslaught of encouragement from my Facebook friends and family, who said, "You should write a book." After hearing that for years, I finally sat down to attempt such a feat. And a feat it has been. I have to say that I had no clue how to write a book. For the past five years, I have been posting a few lines or a few thoughts, and encouraging the readers to think on those thoughts and perhaps implement them into their lives. But to pen thousands of words and make it fluid and coherent? Impossible. For me, anyway. I only finished high school with basic-level English. And while I wanted to play every instrument in the band and be on every sports teams I could, English was not my strong suit.

Over the past five years, God has been teaching me how to write, how to pen thoughts in a way that encourages, builds up, and teaches the church, His beloved Bride. I learned to write only what's necessary, leaving out the unnecessary (our world has enough of that). I even learned to love the dictionary. I know, right? To love words and put them into expressions that encourage and enlighten as well as to teach and showcase God's incredible love story is something that I am honored to be able to do, for Him, and now for you. So how did I really go about writing a book? One step at a time. I took favourite books of mine and went over them page by page and duplicated them (without plagiarising), writing down what I needed to do, literally, from cover to cover (cover ideas, dedication, foreword, table of contents, chapters, conclusions; I am not kidding when I say it was literally step by step).

I would have to write another book to share the entire journey up to this point, as I'm in some circles considered a senior (by age, not by behaviour), but I am going to focus on the past ten or so years, that which I learned and grew to love and became passionate about: Jesus, my sweet Jesus. I watched Him transform my life, my path and direction, my heart, my family, and my mind. No longer in bondage. No longer held and imprisoned by lies and deception. No longer overcome by guilt, shame, and condemnation, but walking through my life in Jesus, free. And it's this freedom journey that I can't wait to share with you. From bars of bondage on the dark cell of depression, I am liberated to dance in complete freedom. Free from me. Alive in Him.

Are you ready to embark on my adventure? I can guarantee that you will see yourself in some, part, or all of my story. It is my prayer that you will come away from these pages into your own experience in the transforming power of Holy Spirit, the Word of God, and the beloved Jesus Christ. Let's begin.

Putting Truth in Its Place

It all began for me about seven years ago. I grabbed a book at a second-hand shop, for no other reason than the title caught my eye: *Who Switched off My Brain?* by Dr. Caroline Leaf. Thinking that it was perhaps a mind-over-matter book, I was quick to return it to the shelf. I think I was mistaken on that; I have since found that this book, and some of her other teachings through videos and podcasts, encouraged me and taught me that through the use of science (and other scientific means, which I know nothing about; remember my English grade? Yep: Biology and chemistry followed far behind that with grades of 28 and 32, respectively) that renewing our minds is both scientifically and scripturally proven. It was at this point, this place of knowing that I needed to have my mind renewed, that I prayed a simple prayer: "God, if this is truth, if you desire to renew my mind and it's been proven through science, then I ask that you'd renew my mind right now with this thought." It was right then and there that He did. How do I know? I can honestly say that I have no idea what the thought was that He replaced. He renewed. Right there at my kitchen sink, praying my simple, "God show up and make this happen" prayer, surrendered to all that He had for me, I experienced the switch, the renewing. I was in a state of shock. I tried desperately to recall that thought, but to this day, I'm unable to remember what it was. To God be all the glory.

What changed? What brought about this altering, this renewal? Was it just the reading of a book? Listening to some podcasts and teachings? In part, yes, but it was my all-in surrender to all that God had for us in His Word, the incredible blessings and revelations. My thoughts and heart began to change, indeed. No longer did I see all of this as some distant, unattainable process, journey, or faith walk. Now, as they say, it was personal. So personal that I tattooed it on my left arm. Oh, don't think I ran off and got a full sleeve with many quotes from Dr. Caroline's book, but rather one word that encompassed not only my journey, but the One to whom this book is dedicated: my Beloved, Jesus.

So what was my heart and mind awakening to? What was so

attractive that I found myself desiring, longing for more and more? It was my understanding of Jesus, of God. No longer was I viewing time and relationship with Him as "religious formal duty" but rather one filled with intimacy and expectations, friendships, and tea parties. Tea parties? Oh, yes, my friend; tea parties. What began as a visit over tea has become a relationship established on God's deep and unfailing love and my falling in love more and more with Him; sometimes literally moment by moment.

Julia Walda

If you have been saved and have been promised eternal life, but like I once did, you still feel trapped in bondage of any kind, this book is for you.

Growing up, I didn't understand what it truly meant to believe in Christ or to have a relationship with Him. I was a church kid, so I basically inherited faith from my parents as I was growing up. Church wasn't necessarily something I wanted to attend, but more often than not, you would find me there on Sunday. After all my years of attending church, I can count on one hand the number of times I had an encounter with God, and even then, I had no idea what that meant. It wasn't until I encountered Jesus for the first time in university that I finally gave my entire heart to God (not to a church) and began my intimate pursuit of Jesus Christ.

One night, I had a dream about dying and seeing heaven; I encountered the real and tangible love of God and woke up the following morning changed. I began reading a King James Version (KJV) Bible and began to uncover truths about life with God that I had never known. I began to read about a mission (the salvation of the world) handed down to me by my Father to reconcile His beloved children back to Himself through Jesus. I began to read of miracles, the Holy Spirit, and radical believers who were recklessly in love with Jesus, to the point of death. It was no longer Sunday school stories or principles I was once taught as a child; it was life itself. A life lived full of the Holy Spirit, with gifts and offices of ministry, with supernatural power and unimaginable promises. It was no longer legalistic, boring, or just being a good person; it was my created purpose in Jesus, my very existence.

I wish I had known when I was a child what I know now. I wish I had known that church was never meant to be a structured, institutionalised building. I wish I had known that I was the church; that I played a vital role in the salvation of others and the edification of my brothers and sisters in Christ. And how I wish I had known I was a brand-new creation. Not theoretically. Not once I die in my earthly body. And not partially. I am and will always be a brand-new creation in Jesus. Born no longer of man, but of the Spirit of God, where Jesus and I became one through His Holy Spirit inside of my heart, the very life force of my existence. I wish I had known that as a new creation, I had freedom from the bondage and power of sin, that I could say no to sin, always. I wish I had known that as a new creation, I had authority over lies and that the promises God speaks of in the Bible are literal truths about me. I wish I had known that this rebirth into the family of God wasn't just a nice saying, but that I would actually become the offspring of God. That's right. If God, in a human sense, had children, those children are us. Mind-blowing.

These are all things I wish I knew, and these are things I pray you begin to understand in your own life. These spiritual truths are just as real as any natural law you see working around you (if not more real than them). The promises God speaks of in His Word are more real than gravity. The words He uses to describe you and define you are more real than the very food you eat for dinner. The way He loves you is greater than the magnificent beauty of creation, and He created it all for you.

I will be honest: I had no intentions of writing this book alongside my mother-in-law. This was something God had been speaking over her for years and something I watched her begin to pursue this past year. It wasn't until one night, when she asked me what I honestly thought about the book and her process, that God aligned us to work together.

The beautiful thing about this entire process is the fact that I have been on this journey with her for nearly two and a half years, before this book was even a prospect. Dawn and I spent many mornings together, talking about our journey with God and what He was teaching us. We would talk about identity, the renewing of the mind, the practical side of it, and our intimacy with God. She spent many years learning the bulk of this book simply by herself with the Lord. She saw all of these things played out in her personal experiences with God, as she sought Him earnestly.

The teaching side of things (that is, the theological, biblical side) is where I come in.

Aside from physically writing and editing the bulk of the book, I was given the honor of assisting Dawn in teaching this valuable life lesson on the renewing of the mind and all that it includes. For myself, I spent a lot of time learning the scriptural truths and revelations behind these things, while she watched as the Holy Spirit revealed them in her own life in a different way. Still through scripture and still through intimacy with God, but we all have different gifts, which is why this works so beautifully.

Dawn offers her personal experiences, metaphoric insight, and the practical tools she used as she encountered the life-changing truths of the Bible. I simply offer those same general ideas in a more in-depth understanding, all to ensure you walk away confident as you pursue God and the renewing of the mind in your own life.

So together, Dawn and I want to invite you into our journey. To a place of sweet intimacy. Listen as Dawn begins the journey at her kitchen table over a hot cup of tea:

"Company is coming." These three words can send anyone into an excited frenzy: cleaning the house, moving things around, and preparing the table with your grandmother's china (unless, of course, you don't enjoy visitors; if that's the case, then get learnin' because

Putting Truth in Its Place

company's coming). Or perhaps you've been taken by surprise by a spouse's comment, "Oh, I forgot to tell you, but we have company coming today at two." To which you reply, "What time is it now?" (If they're wise, they will be running down the hall to get the vacuum all while quietly saying, "Um, it's one.") This was sort of how my "company's coming" notification came.

It was a regular weekday back in 2018; the boys (my husband, John, and son) were away for the day at Bible college, and I was home alone. I had no special plans for the day, maybe hit up a thrift store later, puttering around, and cleaning. I had just finished the dishes when a thought seemed to pass through my mind: *You're having company today.* Company? I didn't even know anyone at the time to have company with (we had only been living in our college town for a year).

I pondered the potential company for a moment or two and thought that maybe God was referring to my father-in-law, as he was the only one I could imagine coming to visit unannounced. I assumed this because he often made deliveries to our city; so maybe he was planning on coming for a visit. This was the only logical outcome I could imagine.

However, amidst my confusion, I obeyed the Holy Spirit and began preparing a tea party for my soon-to-be guest. What is even more interesting is that at this point, John and I were on a sugar fast, which meant no sugary desserts or pastries should be in the house. But it just so happened that prior to the impromptu tea date with who-knows-who, I had been impressed to purchase two single serve desserts that were now sitting fresh and ready in the freezer (the perfect addition to the tea party). What are the odds? Pretty good, considering there are no coincidences with God.

So upon God's odd request, I got the house ready. I steeped the tea. I put the two desserts on a china plate from my husband's nanny. And I completed the table with two of the sweetest teacups from my hutch. Seeing that it was now two o'clock, I asked God the seemingly obvious question: "So where is my company? Who's coming for tea today?"

Whispering to my heart, He replied, "Sit down. You're having tea with Me today."

Two

Introduction to the Renewing of the Mind

> Our purpose is to have you look at basing your
> life entirely off the truth of the Word.

There is a plague within the body of Christ: a lack of freedom. The very thing Christ died for seems to be misinterpreted and reassembled to mean something other than it truly is—a mindset that says we are free but only "somewhat" free. This freedom is limited to a mere positional freedom in the eyes of God, and not a literal spiritual liberation that applies to all aspects of our new life and mind in Christ. This partial freedom narrative states that Jesus only died for freedom from judgement, sin, and hell. It states that we have been forgiven, thus freed from God's wrath and impending judgement, and granted yet another freedom: eternal life. It states that you have been given the golden ticket to eternal life, but only upon death.

In this frame of understanding, you're surviving until one day you can thrive because of the mercy of God and the sacrifice of His Son—the end. There is no here-and-now freedom for those of us who face mental battles every day in the form of things like anxiety, depression, habitual sin, and lack of identity. Because of this, freedom has become an elusive and unattainable concept, continually affirmed by our daily experiences. They do not reflect an everyday, practical freedom, only those that will come at the end of our days.

If this narrative of freedom is true, then it's understandable why one would feel bound and trapped by thoughts of depression and anxiety, a continual struggle with sin, and a lack of identity, as it would imply that Christ is not involved in such subjects.

But what if I can rewrite that narrative? What if that partial freedom narrative is not even true? For Jesus says, "The thief comes only to steal, and kill, and destroy; I came so that they may have life and life abundantly" (John 10:10 ESV). Did you get that? Abundantly.

It's not an empty bucket. It's not partial, lacking, or incomplete, but overflowing. It's not one day, but every day; it's life itself.

This incredible and life-changing reality of complete freedom applies directly to what has crippled the minds of the bride of Christ—things like anxiety, depression, habitual sin, and a lack of identity.

These pressing and extremely relevant concepts that plague even the most devout Christians, to the point of physical debilitation and even a medical diagnosis, are exactly what my heart longs to address in the pages of this book (again as seen through the frame of reference as written in the disclaimer).

Together, we will address this lie, no matter how true it may seem, as we dissect the Word of God and allow it to shape our lives around the truth of Jesus Christ and the full freedom He died for.

My direct intention for this book is to awaken people to their God-given identity and to liberate them to see the truth for themselves and break free from the bondage of deception, lies, and deadly thoughts that have blinded the bride of Christ. Oh, don't tune me out yet; don't just assume this is another one of those books, because it's not. I lived it. I walked a similar path in a different pair of shoes. I saw how the lies of the devil can trap my mind and my body, causing me utter mental and physical debilitation, which screamed so loudly I was seemingly not free in the confines of my own mind.

But here I stand today, free. Not just from hell, not just to attain eternal life (although I am truly grateful for that), and not just to stand acquitted on the day of judgement. No sirree; whoever the Son sets free is free indeed. And today, my beloveds, I am free—daily.

Throughout this book, my desire is to teach you how to use your tool belt of resources to live in freedom; tools like intimacy with God, putting truth in its place, intentionality, and more. These tools are ones I personally discovered and successfully applied to my own life and my daughter-in-law's, which enabled me to walk in ever-increasing freedom and intimacy with God (something I lacked for many years). These resources stem from my understanding of the Holy Scriptures, my fellowship with the Holy Spirit and His leading, and intentionally partnering with God to believe and act on what He has said. Everything I have learned has helped build up my foundation in Christ as a child of God, and I am confident they can help you do the same. And not only do I desire to make you aware of these tools, but I also want to show you how to use them at any time, whenever you may need them.

These tools I will be sharing are readily available for those who hunger and thirst for righteousness; they are derived mainly from the Word of God itself through point-blank scriptures and divine revelation of said scriptures—something that is available to all of us. Because we are addressing that of the mind and the belief system we hold onto, this tool belt we are discussing is mainly conceptual. That means it's not some physical belt you buy with the purchase of the book, nor is it something I will ship to you for a fee. No, sir. It is totally free and totally available to anyone, anywhere. They are simply concepts, practical applications, and tools of the mind, tools that enable the practical process of the renewing of the mind.

However, in addressing these concepts, the presence and activation of faith—that is, faith to believe the truth about things unseen—is necessary in even accessing your tool belt and utilising it to its full capacity (Hebrews 11:1). Without faith in these truths or concepts, you cannot and will not walk in your true identity in Christ.

The same goes for intentionality. You must also be intentional with these practices, as you must be dedicated to living in freedom and knowing what it takes to remain free. Of course, this also includes the strength of the Holy Spirit. But it also takes effort on our behalf as well.

Without faith and intentionality in this journey, it's like needing to go to the well for water, thinking you have a hole in your bucket (dear Liza), so you avoid going all together, causing dehydration. Whereas the truth is, you merely thought there was a hole, when in reality, you had a perfectly whole bucket. Your futile thinking, and your nonexistent desire to find another way, left you dehydrated, when water was available to you the entire time.

This is the reflection of utilising the truth of God's Word but not believing it applies to you, nor seeking out said application.

Quite clearly, this dehydration I mentioned is the same spiritual dehydration you could be experiencing now, which comes from your lack of understanding and believing the truth—the very thing we are going to address. Yay! But Matthew 5:6 (ESV) declares, "Blessed are those who hunger and thirst for righteousness, for they shall be satisfied."

Are you hungry? Are you thirsty? Are you dehydrated? Do you think your proverbial bucket has a hole in it, when it's really intact? And what does the Bible say about those who are indeed hungry and thirsty? "They shall be satisfied." This is a prime example of what it looks like to use your tool belt of resources to actively renew your mind through the Word of God.

Just as I expressed in the previous example, it's the process of filtering our thoughts and beliefs, identifying the lies and misconceptions within those thoughts, and replacing them with God's thoughts and original intended plans and purposes, which have never changed since the beginning.

"For I know the plans I have for you," declares the Lord, "plans to prosper you, and not to harm you. Plans to give you hope and a future. Then you will call upon me and come and pray to me, and I will listen to you!" (Jeremiah 29:11 NIV)

Three

First Things First: Love

Framed and formed in God's love is where your renewal begins.

Before we can address the false narrative of partial freedom, we must first address how the love of God is imperative in experiencing true freedom. For we must first believe that we are loved by God to also believe these glorious freedoms are ours to live by and abide in. This love is displayed in the Bible and evident in the life of Jesus and through the sacrifice of both the Father and the Son.

This love I speak of is not like the feeling most people describe; it can only be understood as God articulates it through the Word. It is not based on feelings or circumstances; it's based solely on the faithfulness of God's testimony of love. It is fully revealed in the sacrifice of God: both the sacrifice of the Father to surrender His Son to death, and the love of Christ to face and endure death Himself.

Even beyond this, we must also meditate upon what preceded this act of true love; that is, the creation of humankind itself and what followed up until Jesus came to earth (and after).

It is easy to overlook such great truths hidden within the Bible, but for the sake of our understanding, we must reference the whole story to also encounter God's whole love. Even before Jesus came to earth, God said to the prophet Jeremiah, "Before I formed you in the womb I knew you, before you were born I set you apart" (Jeremiah 1:5 NIV).

As I mentioned before, scripture says, "'I know the plans I have for you,' declares the Lord, 'plans to prosper you and not to harm you, plans to give you hope and a future'" (Jeremiah 29:11 NIV).

Yet another time, He says, "I have loved you, my people, with an everlasting love. With unfailing love I have drawn you to myself" (Jeremiah 31:3 NLT).

And even before the Fall of man, when Adam and Eve were first created, God looked over all He had made and saw that is was very good (Genesis 1:31).

So many of us have lost (or never known) the gravity of what it means to first be created by God, chosen by Him again and again, even amidst sin and unfaithfulness, and to finally be reconciled to Him through the sacrifice of His very kin, Jesus Christ, so that we might become the righteousness of God. Built into a Holy Priesthood for the sole purpose of knowing God and being known by Him. Doesn't it set your heart ablaze to know you were created by God to be known by Him?

The entire Old Testament, from beginning to the end, is the loving forbearance and patient endurance of God until He could finally, fully redeem us to Himself, through Christ. All this was done amidst our sin, unfaithfulness, and rejection of God; still, we were chosen.

Have you ever contemplated the fact that God knew you were going to turn from Him and would live as a sinner, contrary to His Word, yet still He knew your value and created you in hope of your redemption to Himself? No matter the anguish it would cause Him to see you lost and unfaithful, He still pursued you, even unto death through Christ.

Ephesians 1 lays this out very clearly, stating, "Even before the world was made, God had already chosen us to be his through our union with Christ, so that we would be holy and without fault before him because of His love. God had already decided that through Jesus

Christ he would make us His children—this was his pleasure and purpose" (Ephesians 1:4–5 GNT).

Did you hear that? Did you hear the Father's heart for you, the great pleasure He has always taken in you? He had plans for you before you were even born. Jesus was not a last-ditch effort; He was the intended purpose for us before we were created. Redemption and the love of God were prepared for us in advance. God didn't decide later on, after you had fallen, that you would become His. He decided *before* you were born that you would be chosen in Christ to be His child, His loving and selfless purpose for you, His beloved.

To sum up His great love for you, God knew the price He would have to pay to bear you as His child would be to sacrifice His very Son, who did not deserve to die, and still, He created *you*.

> For God demonstrates his own love for us in this:
> While we were still sinners, Christ died for us.
> (Romans 5:8 NIV)

You do not become loved. You are loved, so you became.

If you fail to understand these truths about God's love for you, lies and bondage from the enemy will continue to wreak havoc upon your mind and thus your life. Meaning that, if you are in any place of bondage, the cure is to now accept this truth that the Bible itself has presented to you.

If you aren't living under the shelter of God's unwavering love, for there is no fear in love but perfect love casts out all fear (1 John 4:18), then what are you living under? What defines your value and your freedom? Is it God's love? If it's not God's love, then it's not true, and it's not freedom.

So how then do we believe and receive God's love? This incredible, unexplainable and unimaginable love? It seems to be something we say flippantly as Christians: "God loves you," but we fail to actually believe it or allow to shape our lives.

Perhaps you are like me, and for years, you could tell others,

"God loves you," but never truly accepted that it applied to you, and in such a life-altering way. This simple yet profound truth that God truly does love us so much that He, the God of the universe, would send His only Son to die for us (who were all sinners at the time) is profound and immensely underappreciate and quite frankly, overlooked.

It is likely because the events of our past and current lives have formed our understanding of what love is; we think about whether we are worthy of God's true love, instead of allowing the simple act of the Father's astounding love to form the truth in our minds, hearts, and lives. The funny thing is, this form of love has always been and always will be the same: unconditional, unwavering, unmatched love of the Father for humankind. But whether this is the form you currently have that supports your foundational beliefs is entirely up to you and how you understand, know, and receive the Word of God. It is one thing to read the Word, and it is another to meditate upon it and believe it, thus allowing the application of its truths in your everyday life.

If you are reading this book and don't understand the love God has for you, that's quite all right because I was there too. It took me over forty years of being a believer in Christ to finally accept and live in the ultimate truth that God loves me.

Until you accept His love, even if you don't yet fully grasp its depth, width, and height, you won't be able to walk in your freedom or identity in Christ.

It is as if the truth of your identity and freedom is the concrete that is to be poured into a framed form, and the love of God is the form that dictates how the concrete will be received. Any form other than the true form that is the love of God will not and cannot retain or support the complimentary concrete that it is to be poured to lay a firm foundation. There is no other form that can create a firm foundation other than that which Christ, the Cornerstone, has already laid through the sacrifice of the Father and the Son.

If this hasn't been your foundational form, take heart because that means your foundation has yet to be laid, and that which you are experiencing right now is simply not complete, nor is it the truth.

This is by no means something to be ashamed of or condemned by, as we must first address the issue to even attack it and form it again. If we never addressed the issue, then you would always stay the same, and it would feel hopeless. But the Father's heart for you is, He *wants* you to know this, and He *wants* to tear down the old form and replace it with the new.

This is, in essence, the renewing of the mind; removing that which is broken, dead, and useless in supporting the promises of God, and creating anew the forms that come directly from the truth of God's Word, designed before the creation of the world to bring freedom and life abundant to you.

So what changed after forty years that caused me to finally believe and receive God's unchanging love for me? It changed when I finally began reading the scriptures and seeing the truths that had been neglected by me for so many years.

How had I always been so ignorant? How had I not understood God's love the way the Bible so clearly depicted it? Why had it taken me so long to receive such a simple revelation? It was because I wasn't reading my Word. I was basing my relationship with God off of everything but the Word alone. I had listened to far too many opinions, experiences, and lies that had infiltrated what I was being taught; not only that, but I chose to believe them. I grew up thinking God was distant from me because I always believed He wasn't a God of intimacy. I revered Him, I respected Him, and I loved Him the way I knew how, but I never grew in intimacy with Him. Quite frankly, I didn't know that was something He desired of me, for I never understood I had a greater purpose in life other than to one day go to heaven. I was simply in the waiting, confident of salvation, but void of the abundance God so promises in His Word for this life. I knew there was something missing but couldn't identify it, thus leaving me in the same state for forty years. I felt trapped. However, I didn't know what I was trapped in, nor did I know where I wanted to go to be free. I knew Jesus was the answer to life, but seeing as there was nothing beyond that ticket to heaven, I never even considered He was the answer to freedom from that entrapment.

It wasn't until a fellow believer challenged me to read my Word that everything began to shift. It didn't happen right away, nor was it an evident shift, but slowly and surely, the Word of God began to permeate my heart and change my mind. Little did I know that everything I had previously mentioned about my forty years of knowing of God was only one small piece to the puzzle of my relationship with Jesus. It wasn't until reading His Word that I stopped viewing God based upon my prior life experience and began seeing His Word for what it truly is: the truth.

This is where I began to see God's love for me in a real, tangible way, that was no longer just reverence and fear, but an intimate love so precious to God that He would die for me. And what was this challenge, you might ask?

About five years ago, a friend of mine lovingly called me out for my lack of Bible knowledge, considering I had graduated from a Bible college and was the wife of a church board member and a member of the worship team. And as you recall, I've been saved for forty years. Seeing as she was accurate in her assessment, I humbled myself to accept that she was correct. Thus, the challenge.

This wonderful friend wisely suggested that I set aside only six minutes a day to read God's Word, hopefully to inspire me to read more. These six minutes consisted of two minutes sitting quietly and collecting my thoughts, two minutes reading a few Bible verses, and two minutes of thanksgiving and praise. That's it. Sound difficult? Most definitely not. In fact, after only six minutes, you realise that isn't really a lot of time to spend with God, and you begin to take a little more time each day you do this. (Not to scare you, but I am currently holding the personal record of three hours and thirty-three minutes.)

Did I choose those specific minutes on purpose? Yes. Do I actually know the time? Nope. I chose it because Jeremiah 33:3

(ESV) says, "Call to me and I will answer you, and will tell you great and hidden things which you have not known."

What seemed to be a simple and attainable task of reading my Bible for only a short while caused me to even notice the word *beloved* riddled throughout the Bible. Had I never intentionally picked up the Word, the Holy Spirit would have never had the chance to show me such beautiful things. He had revealed it to me through others, but without the Bible, there was nothing to confirm its validity.

This word, *beloved,* and this truth of God's love became an evident theme in the scriptures as God Himself was awakening my eyes to the truth that I had never known before. All it took was my simple obedience of reading the Word for six minutes; that gave God the opportunity to speak.

Although I wasn't aware of what was happening during these ever-increasing times of Bible study and prayer, after a year and a half of reading the Word, I began to genuinely seek God and finally receive His love for me. What blows me away is the fact that I had no intention of doing any of this, other than to rise to the challenge of my friend. It was completely the power of the Holy Spirit that changed my heart, as I allowed Him to replace my understanding of what it means to be loved by Him. Thus this newfound yet ancient understanding of God's love was everything I needed in order to start the more intimate process of finding freedom in God's endless promises (something we will touch on later in this book).

It all started from those few minutes set aside for God's Word that unknowingly, through the power of the scriptures and the Holy Spirit, began to stir something in my heart that led to me finally believing in God's unfailing love. This may sound like quite the process to even begin to believe in God's love, but it's imperative. And it is worth it. My only suggestion for you as you embark on your six-minute journey, as I believe it's the best way to begin, is to read the Bible as though it were a story. You don't need to understand the depths of scriptures to understand the overall themes. In reality, you can't force yourself to understand the Bible, for that is the work of the Holy Spirit.

So when you sit down to spend time with the Lord, reading your Word, which is exactly what you're doing, ask Him to reveal His heart, and I promise He will be faithful to your request.

> For the Word of God is alive and powerful. It is sharper than the sharpest two-edged sword, cutting between soul and spirit, joint and marrow. It exposes our innermost thoughts and desires. (Hebrews 4:12 NLT)

Did you get that? *It* exposes. *It* cuts. It is alive. The Word and Holy Spirit are transforming you from the inside out. Your mind being renewed. Not just recycled; made new.

Remember this verse as you embark on this challenge that I now pass on to you.

Four

Intimacy with God

You are loved by God. Chosen by God. Designed by God.

Now that we have been introduced to the truth that God does indeed love us, let us journey the importance of using this truth to cultivate intimacy with Him. In this chapter, I will explain the importance of intimacy and write about why God so desires to be intimate with us. Ultimately, as I hope to show you, the entire reason for our existence is intimacy with our beloved Groom: Christ Jesus.

As I mentioned in the previous chapter, I didn't know that God desired intimacy with me, nor was I aware that it was missing in my Christian walk. That "abundant life" Christ had always promised me was waiting on the other side of simply becoming intimate with Jesus; that is, being *known* by God and *knowing* God.

You may have a few questions leading into this chapter like, what is intimacy? Why do we need intimacy? What is intimacy with God? Why would God desire intimacy with us? Oh, so many questions, and even fewer answers (for me, anyway). A seemingly daunting task of configuring all of these answers to make any type of sense, a kaleidoscope of inconclusives and misunderstoods. That was, until my journey of six minutes, tea parties (remember my invitation to tea in the introduction?), and the securing of my safe place. Little did I know that these simple proactive actions would lead me to the most incredible place of intimacy I find myself today. But don't let me get ahead of myself. Let's tackle the above questions one at a time. This will not only provide understanding for the journey, it will also give us an opportunity to secure the necessary tools in our tool belt.

So what is intimacy? The world's definition and the Bible's definition are polar opposites, much like comparing night and day. It's important that we address both and implement that which is the correct definition, because too often we rely on our human experiences to define that which we believe to be true. More often than not, we base our understanding of God and our interactions with Him off of broken thoughts, and it negatively impacts our relationship with the Lord.

In many cases, our view of intimacy with God is either nonexistent or greatly flawed due to how the world defines *intimacy* and *love*. You may view intimacy as strictly related to sex. Maybe you view it as the close moments of being with a spouse or romantic partner. And maybe the word *intimacy* makes you feel uncomfortable, and it's not something you would ever use to define your relationship with God. I believe that for many of us, intimacy has been widely used to reference sexual acts (whether in marriage or not, with a partner or without); a purely carnal word. I also believe that we rarely use intimacy to refer to precious moments of *knowing* and *being known* by someone, even in a purely nonsexual way. On top of that, when we do refer to intimacy as something sexual, very rarely is the prerequisite a lasting bond and a desire to edify a beloved partner; more often, its simply an overwhelming sexual desire that leads to an action: "being intimate."

I believe that *intimacy* in our generation is much like the term "making love." There are countless songs that use the phrase "making love" or "to make love." Are they actually trying to selflessly love someone? Likely not, as many of these songs speak vulgarly about women and relationships, and often reference a night in the club or a "we just met, let's make love."

As you could likely figure, using any of these definitions of intimacy in regard to a relationship with God is highly inappropriate and quite disturbing. We can all agree that intimacy with God does not mean something that is sexual or carnal. We can likely agree that intimacy with God references that which is spiritual and of the heart, not something of the flesh.

So, considering many of us may be unaware of the true biblical meaning of the word, let's see how God defines *intimacy*. In order to do this, we must first understand the kind of relationship God desires with us. We can all relate to defining the relationship with a boyfriend/girlfriend, or moving out of the friend zone into actually dating. Many of us can also relate to the first time we ever talked about marriage with our future spouse. All of these moments are imperative to building a relationship, as we must first understand the parameters of our interaction. Of course, a friendship is different from a dating relationship, and a dating relationship is not the same as a marriage. So what has God defined our relationship with Him as? So many beautiful things.

First, God has adopted us as children; He is our Father, and we are His children. This relationship looks like guidance, protection, and the inexplicable bond between parents and their children, like when children run to their father's arms after a bad dream or during a heavy thunderstorm. Unfortunately, this relationship is also skewed in our society and can only be understood in that which God has fundamentally designed Fatherhood to be. I won't go into this too much. However, I will recite two precious verses from the Word of God that echo this glorious truth:

> For you have not received the spirit of bondage again to fear; but you have received the Spirit of adoption, whereby we cry, Abba, Father. (Romans 8:15 NLT)

> The Lord himself watches over you! The Lord stands beside you as your protective shade. The sun will not

> harm you by day, nor the moon at night. The Lord keeps you from all harm and watches over your life. The Lord keeps watch over you as you come and go, both now and forever. (Psalm 121:5–8 NLT)

The second definitive relationship we have with God is the Bride of Christ. Of course, there are others commonly referenced, such as friendship with God, being servants or priests of the Lord, but for the sake of understanding intimacy, being Christ's bride is the most imperative. So what does it mean to be the Bride of Christ if we are not referring to any form of sexual relations? Well, let's see what the Bible says.

In the Old Testament, God often refers to His relationship with Israel (His chosen people), as being their husband or their lover (again, not sexually).

> For your Creator will be your husband; the LORD of Heaven's Armies is his name! He is your Redeemer, the Holy One of Israel, the God of all the earth. (Isaiah 54:5 NLT)

In Ezekiel, the Lord addresses Jerusalem for their detestable practices and recounts His marriage covenant with them, although they were unfaithful:

> Later I passed by, and when I looked at you and saw that you were old enough for love, I spread the corner of my garment over you and covered your naked body. I gave you my solemn oath and entered into a covenant with you, declares the Sovereign LORD, and you became mine. (Ezekiel 16:8 NIV)

The covenant He is referring to that made Jerusalem His is a marriage-type covenant. Again, He confirms this with Hosea: "In that day, declares the Lord, you will call Me 'my Husband', and no longer call Me 'my Master'" (Hosea 2:16–17 NIV).

If that's not enough, just look at the imagery riddled throughout the New Testament that declares we are the Bride of Christ. Paul speaks of his passion for the church and their marriage to Christ by saying, "For I am jealous for you with the jealousy of God himself. I promised you as a pure bride to one husband—Christ" (2 Corinthians 11:2 NLT).

And finally, in Revelation, John writes of the "marriage supper," the feast that follows our marriage to Christ:

> "Let us be glad and rejoice and give Him glory, for the marriage of the Lamb has come, and His wife has made herself ready." And to her it was granted to be arrayed in fine linen, clean and bright, for the fine linen is the righteous acts of the saints. Then he said to me, "Write: 'Blessed are those who are called to the marriage supper of the Lamb!'" And he said to me, "These are the true sayings of God." (Revelation 19:7–9 ESV)

Hopefully, you can agree with me that the scriptures do indeed call us to be the Bride of Christ and for God to be our husband. Now that we have defined the relationship, what does Biblical intimacy with our husband, Jesus Christ, look like?

What happens after we get married? We start getting to truly know our spouse. We start living with them. With Christ, this is our very eternity, for the Word of God says, "This is eternal life, that they may know You, the only true God, and Jesus Christ whom You have sent" (John 17:3 ESV).

What is so important here is the word *know*, as the Greek word used here in the original translation is *ginōskōsin*. Ginōskōsin means to know, to perceive, to understand, and according to Bibletools.

org, it's also a Jewish expression for intercourse between a man and a woman.

Does it make sense now why *intimacy* often refers to something sexual? But even before someone could use it as an expression for intercourse, it simply means to know, understand, and perceive. One could say to *truly* know, to *truly* understand, and to *truly* perceive.

Much like the imagery between a man and a woman in marital intercourse, only the two who are involved in the experience know the intimate places of their spouse. Only they have seen, experienced, and been a part of the most vulnerable aspects of their beloved.

This is such a beautiful expression, that we may know Jesus. And on top of that, the simple act of knowing Him intimately is eternal life.

Do you know Christ as your husband? Do you know Him intimately? Do you understand His heart, His mind, His desires? Do you know Him in a way where just the two of you spend time together, rejoicing in each other's presence? Or do you simply know *of* God?

Now that we have put truth in its place and unpacked what intimacy with God can look like, let's address the necessity and practicality of this intimacy.

Continuing on with the analogy of marriage, intimacy, when seen through the correct biblical perspective, implies that there is a need to spend time and invest in our relationship with God, as well as understanding the One with whom we are meeting. How, you may ask? Remember the approach to the tea party? When God invited me to have tea, we must remember that it was not because He needed time to get to know me; He created me. He already knows my frame. Psalm 103 says, "He knows how we are formed, he remembers that we are dust" (Psalm 103:14 NIV).

His desire to be with me was so that I may be with Him, so that I may know Him. That is real intimacy: the mutual knowing. He already knowing me, and me knowing Him, in all ways.

If you are anything like I was, knowing of God may seem to

be enough. For me, there was never an urgency to understand Him more, let alone a desire to become intimate with God.

In my eyes, how could I ever do or need that when my view of God was one of distance and anger? My veiled heart and mind did not see any need for becoming intimate with Him; I remained satisfied with what I knew. Before understanding the Word and intimacy, I believed many lies and battled countless thoughts that said, "Not good enough," "There's no such thing as intimacy with God," or "I'm not worthy of God's love, let alone His time."

These thoughts had no scriptural basis, of course; they were obviously inspired by the accuser: Satan. But I did not know that. And maybe you don't, either. Maybe you're still in the place of battling lies such as those aforementioned, and you need to put some truth in its place. Worry not. The truth is exactly what we are addressing. Because I finally began to uncover the incredible truth of God's love for me. And where? The Bible, of course.

The Bible is God's love letter to us, His very breathed words of intimacy, where He speaks of His unconditional love for me and for you. When we fail to be in the scriptures, we fail to understand His great love. This leaves us veiled (like I was) and wandering in the darkness of lies and misunderstandings.

If our thoughts remain unaddressed and unassessed, we are left in a state of indecision and will remain disconnected from the Lord; rendered powerless in our pursuit. Or worse yet, like me, we may even fail to see the need for a pursuit.

In chapter 3, we established the truth of God's incredible love for us. He created us for relationship, fellowship, and purpose. Since the beginning of Creation, He has desired fellowship and intimacy, to walk in the garden with Him. And now, to have tea time, to be surrounded in the beauty of relationship, to be fully known, just as God fully knows us.

You see, when God invited me to the tea party, it wasn't because of what I had done or what I had to offer Him; it was because of who I was in His eyes. I did not have to work to receive His invitation; He freely extended it to me, as I was already accepted by Him. That day when I heard Him speak of the impending tea party, I had prepared the house, the tea, and the table setting, all under the pretense that I was having human company. In a natural perspective, all I had to offer at this party was my natural ability to create a welcoming atmosphere; aside from that, there was nothing special I could give. But God was not awaiting the tea at all; He was simply awaiting me.

Now, if I had known it was God who was joining me for tea from the beginning, my preparations would have looked a lot different, but of course He knew that. Not knowing the "who" while preparing the party set me in the perfect place to receive the Lord's invitation. I did not have time to sit around and ponder whether I was qualified or prepared to sit for tea with the Lord. I just assumed whoever was coming over was a friend; there was no need to feel inadequate or unworthy. Thus, when the I heard the Holy Spirit invite me to "come," as it was He and I who were set to have tea, I didn't have time to second-guess myself or His invitation.

For some people, the thought of sitting alone with God produces many accusing thoughts that tend to keep them from even approaching the Lord.

Maybe they are saying, "There's no way I can come. There is too much stuff. I cannot comprehend why God would want to be with me." I would even go as far to say that some of you believe God desires to spend time with others, but you do not feel that applies to you. Maybe you don't even like spending time with yourself. Maybe you feel sinful, are filled with shame and guilt, and can hardly lift your eyes to such a holy throne. And maybe you feel even more disqualified because your heart seems to condemn you for even thinking such a way, further affirming the lie. All of these thoughts can build up or reinforce the walls we have built between us and God. Right now, it may even seem like there is a towering wall, built to cage you in and keep God out. The truth is, much like the veil that was over my eyes that kept me from understanding God's love

Putting Truth in Its Place

for me (and all the other truths about my identity in Christ), this wall you may feel is also a veil.

It may seem heavy and solid; it may not be something you'd describe as a veil, but I am here to reassure you that it is simply a veil. It does not need heavy machinery, power tools, or strong men to tear it down, piece by piece. It needs the loving hand of your Groom to lift the thin layer of fabric up over your head and away from your eyes. You are the Bride of Christ, and Jesus has vowed to lift the veil. Actually, Jesus already tore the veil when He died for you on the cross. But for some of us, by choice or lack of knowledge, that veil still rests over our eyes. My beloved friends, it is not a wall. It is simply a veil of lies that Jesus wants to remove from your eyes as you let His truth penetrate your hearts and, most importantly, your minds. Go and put this in your tool box, my friends. This is one you will access over and over again. Let us continue to unpack the truth about God's desire for intimacy with us, as my ultimate desire is for you to experience your own tea parties with Jesus.

You see, when God asked me to spend time with Him that day, it was not because of anything I had done. If I had known God was attending, it would have been easy for me to take a quick look inward and find all the reasons why I was unworthy for His holy presence. It's quite sad, actually, because as my daughter-in-law recounts in her past encounters with Jesus, she used to be in shame and guilt for twenty minutes whilst praying with the Lord. For whatever reason (lies), she couldn't even rest in God's presence; she felt this awful weight of shame and guilt, and a need to "pray harder" until she worked her way up the holy ladder to Jesus.

Maybe this is true for some of you reading today. Maybe you enter into God's presence with overwhelming shame and guilt.

The truth is, that is yet another veil that rests awfully unnoticed over our eyes. In later chapters, we will unpack this truth, the truth that states you are holy, worthy, and righteous, but for now, just take heart and know that you will not always be in this place.

Now that I know this truth, I realise these reasons that previously disqualified me were no reasons at all, as Jesus had already cleansed me and made me new. He had already decided I was worthy.

As we can recall, the six minutes in the Word began to teach me the character of God, His very nature. But thank God it did not end there. I also began to see who I was, who God declared me to be in Christ: "for it is no longer I who live, but Christ who lives in me" (Galatians 2:20 ESV).

The words I read in the Bible are the very thoughts of God that pertain to His intentions and His created purposes for me. Although I once lived under the veil of lies and misunderstandings that came from my life experiences, I finally began to comprehend that the truth of God's Word was actually the truth. It was real, just as real as the chair I am sitting on whilst I write. Just as real as the food I will eat for lunch. I began to read, see, and finally comprehend what God declares and even sings over me. I let the very declarations of the Bible dictate how I viewed God and how He viewed me, and it transformed my intimacy with the Lord; it actually birthed the very intimacy that has strengthened my understanding even more.

Verses like "'I know the plans I have for you,' declares the Lord, 'plans to prosper you and not to harm you, plans to give you hope and a future'" (Jeremiah 29:11 NIV).

Let me take a moment and share a practical tool that I personally used with this verse, a glimpse into what your six minutes could look like.

I would begin with contemplating words. Understand individual words. Take a moment to consider the purpose of certain words. Sometimes, a word seems to be highlighted or illuminated, causing me to pause and consider it more fully. Almost like a whisper of "Did you consider this?" Teaching me to pause. Reflect. Contemplate.

Take for instance the words *declare, know, plans*.

These words conjure up, at least for me, action, movement, and intentionality, as though God is being intentional with me, that God was even pursuing me. It was verses and moments like this where I began to see that God desired me. We were not to be separately functioning, with God way over there, and me, in the opposite direction. We were to be connected, and He was the One in the know, and I was the one the world was intended for: "'For I know the plans I have for you,' declares the LORD" (Jeremiah 29:11 NIV). The plans He has for me. The plans He has for you.

You do not make a plan for someone unless you want to be involved; that would just be silly. You also would not make an intricate plan for someone's very life if they weren't of value to you; that would be just as silly. And how on earth did these simple words penetrate my heart in such a life-changing way? All it took was the Holy Spirit and a dictionary.

A dictionary? A dictionary. I'm sure we can all agree that the Holy Spirit reveals things to us as we read. But a dictionary? Yes. I don't want to jump too far ahead here, but I can guarantee you that a dictionary is a useful tool to have in your tool box. (Even now, I anticipate a hard copy one for Christmas from my secret Santa; in the meantime, an electronic dictionary will suffice.)

When dissecting Jeremiah 29:11 with the Holy Spirit and a dictionary, I first stumbled across the word *you* in the phrase "'For I know the plans I have for *you*,' declares the Lord." Did you catch my emphasis on the word "you"? It doesn't say, "I know the plans I have for everyone else. Everyone who has it all together. Others." It's direct and quite precise: you. Oh, such a personal verse that screams of His intentional intimate purposes for us, for you. This alone makes me dance internally (also, truth be told, physically). Just this understanding of God declaring His plans for me personally can set me dancing all day. (Yep, I have even been known to dance in the grocery store, a parking lot, and even a hardware store. Truth speaking right there; just ask my family and friends.)

I wish I could express to you the looks of concern I get from them when these seemingly strange and childlike dances occur. Their concerns are not mine as I dance about, for I am overcome with joy. I know God created me with purpose, and I feel giddy about it. His very hands sculpted me, formed me. And why? Because He has a purpose for me; He has plans for me.

All of this is so very important for us as children of God to understand, because it fulfills our inherent need for love and that something we can't quite put our finger on. We desperately need to know that the Father loves us and that He wants to be intimate with us. We must let the truth of God's Word completely lift the veil from our eyes and allow the freedom of what God actually says about us to reign in our lives. This is the freedom that comes from knowing you are loved by God. Chosen by God. Designed by God. The very freedom Jesus died for. The same freedom that releases you from the shackles of lies and fastens in place the belt of truth.

Wow; your tool box is becoming harder to close already. Can you imagine what it's going to look like when you are done the book? Perhaps you're going to need a trip to the local hardware store to buy one of those large red rolling ones. I know I'd be down for a shopping trip like that right now.

Five

Intimacy with God: The Practical Application

✦✦✦✦✦

Maybe you don't think you need it, maybe you don't feel worthy for it, maybe you won't know what it looks like ... you need intimacy with your Groom.

Continuing in our journey to freedom and *knowing Go*d (all revealed in the person of Jesus Christ), let's tackle some practical tools that will help you seek the Lord in your daily life!

When I was on my own journey to freedom, some five-odd years ago, before I even understood the depths of God's love and the relationship I could have with Him, I thought the freedom I was looking for would be found in the dance studio. I thought I needed a little creative expression in my life to bring me to a place of carefree living (or, in this case, dancing). But what I thought would be found in a few dance classes filled with missteps and hip-hop music was actually found in Jesus through intimacy with God. What I had longed for wasn't fulfilled on a physical dance floor (or anywhere else, for that matter). My freedom was found in understanding the truth of the scripture that declared God's incredible love for me. The same scripture declares Jesus's selfless sacrifice and triumphant resurrection, all for us. The fact of the matter is this: You need intimacy with God to find true freedom, and you need to start pursuing Him by reading your Bible.

Maybe you don't think you need it, maybe you don't feel worthy for it, maybe you don't even know what it looks like. Whatever the case, as your sister in Christ, I can assure you that you need intimacy with your Groom; you need intimacy with Jesus. Maybe you don't have all the answers for your questions yet. Maybe, like me, you're not even sure what questions need answering; that's okay. Only the Holy Spirit can truly answer them.

All I have done is offer the truth of scripture and how it has applied to my life, in hopes that the Holy Spirit will illuminate a hunger and an excitement for what is also available for you. I urge you with zeal in my heart to be honest and real about what's going on in your heart. You can count yourselves blessed, as you aren't the one exposing your thoughts to the world (as I am right now), but you *must* expose your thoughts to God. He already knows your thoughts, but it's for you, not for God. You must first address that there is a problem to even find a solution, and that solution being the Word of God and understanding His love for you.

Without honestly assessing where you are at, you may never realise that where you are is leaving you feeling empty and unfulfilled, even as a believer.

For forty years, I searched for something I didn't know I needed and, worse yet, didn't know existed. I had heard preached and sung the instruction of "Read your Bible, pray every day, and you'll grow, grow, grow," but that's all it was to me. Another of the "dos" to add to my spiritual to-do list. But truly I give praise to God for His incredible revelation of His love toward me, as I no longer see my faith journey through a veil of dos and don'ts, but rather I stand confident in my relationship with Him. I now know that He created me for purpose. And if He created all the universe with such purpose, I must have incredible purpose as well.

Expose the Lie, Declare the Truth (Jesus School 2019)

Now, moving forward into maintaining the practical application of intimacy, you must first remember to address any lies that seem to keep you from Him and find the corresponding truths that actually draw you closer to Him. As a friend once explained to me, "Expose the lie, declare the truth."

Any time you hear or feel a lie, stop dead in your tracks, process the thought, and expose that lie! Lies can be really easy to spot because they cause shame, condemnation, and guilt, none of which come from God. And it will not line up to the truths of scripture. Whenever you sense something is keeping you from God, don't just let it pass; address it. Expose that lie. And most importantly, find the corresponding truth. Get into the scriptures ASAP (helpful hint here: get some cue cards and write the following scriptures out and put them in your tool box; I guarantee you will need them again).

If you feel unloved, find a verse like "Yes, I have loved you with an everlasting love; therefore with lovingkindness I have drawn you to myself" (Jeremiah 31:3 NLT).

If you feel unworthy, find a verse like "Are not five sparrows sold for two copper coins? And not one of them is forgotten before God. But the very hairs of your head are all numbered. Do not fear therefore; you are of more value than many sparrows" (Luke 12:6–7 ESV).

If you feel ashamed, find a verse like "So now there is no condemnation for those who belong to Christ Jesus. And because you belong to him, the power of the life-giving Spirit has freed you from the power of sin that leads to death" (Romans 8:1–2 ESV).

If you feel like you're trying to make God love you, remember "But God showed his great love for us by sending Christ to die for us while we were still sinners" (Romans 5:8 NLT).

It is imperative to reflect on these truths when you become overwhelmed with guilt and shame, or if you feel as though you cannot approach God. Anything that keeps you from approaching

God is absolutely not from God because, as I explained, He created us to be with Him. Truly. And if you don't think you're qualified for intimacy with God, go back and reread chapter 4 until you start believing the biblical truths I have laid out for you. By reading and allowing the Word of God to penetrate your heart and mind, as I have, you will no longer be bound in a place of unknowns and lies. But like me, you may even begin to dance. There's plenty of room on God's dance floor.

Let me encourage you right now to give thanks to God for offering and extending to you His invitation to "come." No matter what you may believe about your relationship with God, I urge you to allow Him to speak into your heart. Allow Him to teach you His ways and His love. Allow the Holy Spirit to illuminate what is absolutely true about you. Don't fret if you don't understand right away; it takes time for the Spirit to work in your life, even though it can also happen in an instant. But you must first give God the opportunity to change your perspective, and you must humble yourself to believe that your perspective needs to be changed. You must let go of any damaging beliefs, even if they have been with you for as long as you can remember. I pray too that the Holy Spirit allows you the grace to let go and let God, to assess and address, to expose the lies and put truth in its place.

The Secret Place

As displayed in the tea-party story, it was God who invited me to sit with him and have tea: something so simple, yet clearly of value to Him. He felt it of value to create a space where He and I could talk and fellowship, as friends would. It was less formal, less religious, and revealed the heart of God for me as His beloved: two lovers, sitting together for tea.

As previously explained, God began revealing His love for me in the Word, but He revealed this love for me in a practical way through these precious moments drinking tea.

I could sense His presence as He sat with me at the table, drinking his tea (well, not really, although I hoped one day He would) and talking with me, face to face. It was a beautiful tea party with Jesus because I wasn't journaling (as I so often do); I wasn't sharing with Him a laundry list of my needs, and I wasn't expecting anything from Him except for His presence. It was beautiful and peaceful, and it overwhelmed my heart as I pondered the value of His desire to meet with me in such a "me" way. He knew me. He knows me. And He knows you too.

Ultimately, this *is* the secret place: being known by God and knowing God. Some days, it looks like tea parties; it often looks like journaling, and yet some days, it's a constant awareness that at any moment, I can go to my God, my beloved Jesus, and be in His presence.

I can be in line at the grocery store, driving my car, or sitting quietly while looking out at the picturesque waterfront. No matter the day or the circumstance, I can know my God is with me and that I am His beloved. These moments with God are meant to be unhindered by lies and shame; they are accessible at any time.

Some of you may be experiencing hindrances in your intimate time with Jesus because you struggle to approach God boldly, without fear or worry. I myself used to battle guilt and shame as I came before the Lord in any facet, and there were many days it actually kept me away from Him. But once I overcame those lies and understood the truth (as I keep mentioning), only then did I find freedom to approach the throne of grace with boldness and confidence, knowing that my God would be there for me always.

So whether you are prepared and ready for the tea party or are still unsure of your standing with God, there is hope yet to building up this secret place, as this book so declares.

As aforementioned, my secret place can consist of a few daily practices: journaling, reading, driving, and so on. However, there is also a physical secret place that we can create to help us as we seek the Lord.

The Physical Secret Place

Although spending time with Jesus does not always require a literal place, it is good to have that favourite place where you know you can retreat to and find peace to seek the Lord. Mine has transitioned and changed over the years, mostly because we have moved three times in three and a half years. Okay, not mostly because of our demographic changes; it was because we moved. That being said, I did intentionally seek out a secret place in each of our homes. The first one was in our glorious front sunroom. Oh, how I miss that sweet place. My second was in my chair, positioned just right to capture and soak in the beauty of the morning sunrise. And now in our third home? My special secret place rotates. So I suppose that alone makes it special, right? No matter where I station myself, no matter the time of day (I love the wee hours of the morning, as the house is super quiet), I love to read, write, pray, and just be in the place to meet with my beloved, Jesus.

Each of you will find, discover, and yes, celebrate your sweet place. For this is a good place to have for moms and dads alike, college students living with roommates, or anyone who desires a physical escape. It doesn't necessarily mean you need to leave the confines of your home to have that place; it can consist of a special chair, a reading nook, or even your backyard: whatever feels like rest when you go there.

For some of you, this place does not yet exist, so based upon my many years of interior design knowledge, I suggest creating a space. That may look like finding a cute chair on the internet and buying it, or decorating a space to make it feel homier, or even cleaning out a spare room to make it your own oasis.

When creating a physical space for seeking Jesus (good for

reading, praying, writing), it's important that it is a desirable space first, an inviting space (this is another practical and useful tool). If it isn't very inviting, it will cause you more tension than joy, as it may begin to feel like a chore, not an escape for you to sit cuddly and cosy with Jesus as you seek Him. It will also feel less peaceful and enjoyable if the space is not homey or styled, as the atmosphere surrounding that area will feel incomplete or "under construction": most certainly not peaceful words.

But remember, these are suggestions, not rules on how to seek Jesus; it is not necessary to redecorate your home simply because I have suggested making a safe space. I am aware that for some people, this isn't even possible. But as a woman who values that which inspires emotion and comfort, even something as simple as a throw blanket or quilt that makes you feel comfort while you seek the Comforter is a good tool. And if you don't see your home as a safe space, a coffee shop, library, park, or wherever else you may desire can be a great retreat when desiring to get alone with God.

What I mean by a safe space is a physical space that invokes peace, tranquility, and rest. For some, this could be a bustling park, full of people and life; for others, it's a secluded cubicle in a library with soft music playing in their headphones. And for still others, it's while their children are playing on the floor, as they take sips of their lukewarm coffee.

When my daughter-in-law lived in downtown Ottawa, she found her safe space in coffee shops. She wasn't able to make her home that space, so she sought it out in areas around her and enjoyed different settings, cultures, and atmospheres at the same time. It was an adventure each day to find a new coffee shop and sit with the Lord while drinking a cup of coffee.

For you, these may be more practical ways of seeking the Lord and making that time for Him. Of course, we don't go on a date with our spouses every night, but we do spend time with them daily as we go about our lives. This is the same with Jesus. This safe space can be a part of your everyday routine; some days, it will be a special date with God that allows your mind to rest and focus solely on Him. Either way, it is possible to spend time with Jesus every day, even if it doesn't look like sitting down and being still for hours on end. Because the beautiful thing is, Jesus is with you at all times, every day. He never leaves, never takes a break, and is always closer than your very breath. He is the Spirit of God that lives within you.

All this to say, there are times for tea parties and times for simply knowing, sitting in, dwelling in our understanding of who we are to Him. Both stem from understanding God's infinite love for His beloved children, and both are accessible to us. My dear friends, let's just sit and rest in this truth: We are His beloved, called by name to sit in and dwell in His presence. Oh, let the sweet wind of His presence sweep over you right now … whoosh.

Six

"I Am Who You Say I Am"

I am His handiwork; He wrote the instruction
manual on who I am and how I function.

Who are you? Are you defined by what others say or think about you? Does what you do define who you are? Do you know your identity as a new creation in Jesus, or do you think that even post-salvation, you are still the same old person?

> *Who You Say I Am*, by Hillsong
> I am chosen,
> not forsaken.
> I am who You say I am.
> You are for me,
> not against me.
> I am who You say I am.

I love that last line: "I am who You say I am." Seems rather declarative, don't you think? A rather definitive statement that you truly are all that God says you are. When I read these lyrics, I like to think that the songwriters, Reuben Morgan and Ben Fielding, had a clear, sure, and certain understanding of what it was they were singing. I believe their intentions were to lead others into that same revelation also. However, it's easy to simply sing a song like this without ever allowing the words to penetrate our hearts. The real victory is to believe that they are true and to express them as a declaration; that takes faith and knowing.

I know that for me, I had a very limited grasp when it came to understanding all that God had spoken over me. I also failed to believe that what He said about me was actually true, as the God who created me obviously knows who I am. I am His handiwork. He wrote the instruction manual on who I am and how I function. However, for so long, I listened to other voices who had never read God's instruction manual for me, and I foolishly received their opinions as truth. It seemed so easy to base my identity off other people's opinions and my own experiences, but to believe God at His word? That was much harder.

After some consideration, it does make sense that the God who created me certainly does have the right to make me into anything He desires. For God says in Jeremiah 18:6 (NLT), "as the clay is in the potter's hand, so are you in my hand." Clearly the potter dictates the form of the clay, and not the other way around: "Shall what is formed say to him who formed it, 'Why did you make me like this?'" (Romans 9:20 NIV).

So how is it that God has made us? How does He define us? Well, if everything I have written thus far about God and His love is true, then we can also assume that everything He says about us is full of love, purpose, and value.

So is our identity actually ours to dictate, as some would say it is, or is it dictated by God? Does the painting tell the artist its meaning? Or does the artist dictate the meaning of the painting? In the same way, God is the only One who can and should dictate our identity. Is the declarative narrative that we sing (like the song aforementioned) or speak over ourselves that which God declares over us? Or have we conjured up our own conclusions based on the world's ideas and ideals, our experiences, feelings, or veiled understanding of scriptures? We cannot and should not live in any narrative other than

Putting Truth in Its Place

God's written and confirmed words, because anything less than that is a lie. And what do lies lead to? Separation. Disfunction. Agony. Guilt. Shame. Grief. Anxiety. Depression. And who is the author of lies? Well, our enemy, of course. That same devil who is prowling around like a lion, looking for those he can steal, kill, and destroy.

I think it wise to use this next portion to drive headlong into those enemy lies that are playing on repeat in the record player of our minds.

Imagine your mind is a record player, and imagine there are two records you can listen to. The first record is labelled "SKD" (which stands for "Steal, Kill, and Destroy"); you can probably guess who produced that one. That's right, the devil (production by Criminal Records). This particular kind of record album makes you feel many emotions whilst screaming about a thousand different things into your ears all at once. Although its words are aggressive, its tune is catchy and its lyrics relatable.

The second album is far more tranquil and evokes thoughts that bring love, joy, and peace. Its lyrics are gentle and kind; they often sound too good to be true. However, when it is played, it feels like life itself is worth living and reminds you that you are valued and loved. This record is labelled "LMA" ("Life More Abundant"), and its Producer? Jesus Himself.

For me, I had allowed the SKD record to play on repeat because it seemed to be the right fit; it sounded right. As the years went on, the album stayed the same, but the cover kept getting a fresh new update. Although it was just the same old, same old, it felt new, modern, and suitable for me, even as I aged; I just kept buying into its clever marketing and relatable soundtrack. I never realised that this SKD album I had bought into for so long was just a bunch of lies from the enemy, who intended to do just as its title professed: steal, kill, and destroy.

It wasn't until my six minutes in the Word (now 3:33) that I began to realise that this record I was playing was causing me immense harm and wasn't even remotely true. My yearly subscription to this melancholy album had just been a waste of my time; I wasted mental energy on lies that held no merit or value in my life, although at the time, I held them as truth. Once I encountered the songs of truth that God had been singing over me in His Word, I scrapped that dusty old SKD record and began to play on repeat that which God had purposed for me.

As I allowed the scriptures to reveal God's truth to my heart through the Holy Spirit's teaching, I began to hear new songs, love songs. Their unusual yet somehow familiar tunes resonated deep within my heart, causing me to tilt my head and ask, "What is this?" These songs I began to hear were scriptures like:

> "For I know the plans I have for you," says the LORD. "They are plans for good and not for disaster, to give you a future and a hope." (Jeremiah 29:11 NLT)

> You are royal priests, a holy nation, God's very own possession. (1 Peter 2:9 NLT)

> And because of his glory and excellence, he has given us great and precious promises. These are the promises that enable you to share his divine nature and escape the world's corruption caused by human desires. (2 Peter 1:4 NLT)

> Yet now he has reconciled you to himself through the death of Christ in his physical body. As a result, he has brought you into his own presence, and you are holy and blameless as you stand before him without a single fault. (Colossians 1:22 NLT)

I began to play these love songs on repeat. Each purposed note and instrument was comforting, even transformative. Such

Putting Truth in Its Place

profound and liberating declarations caused my eyes to well up with tears, having never heard something so powerful and lovely. Their message was one of hope, life, and love.

I must be honest and admit that their message was not one I believed right away, although in my heart, I felt their words to be true. I didn't believe their declarations over me, but I knew they were doing a work in my life. I couldn't quite describe the depths, characteristics, or specifics of these glorious promises I was hearing, but I knew that this album was indeed LMA. This album was different from the last, as its songs weren't dictated by opinions or experiences, but by One creator, *the* Creator, for me personally and for all of God's beloved children.

It wasn't until I accepted the challenge to read my word and begin the process of applying these declarations to my life personally that I began to believe them. It would have been easy to stay in a place of simply feeling His words instead of finally believing and thus applying them. As I mentioned, it was my six minutes that led me to realise there was more for me in my relationship with God. Those revelations of God's love then led me to spend more time in intimacy with Him, building up our relationship. Ultimately, it was His love and our greater intimacy together that then led to the switch from SKD to LMA.

The switch seemed to happen almost seamlessly as I let the words of the Bible and the love of God move through my heart, as the Holy Spirit transformed me. I didn't have to try; I just had to be available and willing. Like I said, I didn't believe these verses right away. It was my six-minute challenge of just reading the verses that led me to finally seeing and believing. For the Bible says that the Word is alive and active; boy, did I learn this to be true. It was in simply reading these verses that I began to feel my spirit awaken in a new way, thus renewing my mind in the process. But not just renewed: transformed. However, renewal was not the why of my reading, nor did I think I needed a heart change. Even now, I ask myself why I was reading those verses. Why would I read them if there was no desire?

The answer is simple. The Holy Spirit knew I needed an album switch, and it was the Holy Spirit who led me to accept my friend's challenge. It was the Holy Spirit who did all the revealing, and it was the Holy Spirit who, when I partnered with Him, changed my entire life.

It was more likely than not (just kidding; it most certainly was) the Holy Spirit who led you to read this book. And it will be the Holy Spirit who will open your eyes to greater freedom than you could ever imagine, if you allow Him to teach you to renew your mind.

Again, with this word *renew*. I know we've all heard sermons and podcasts on this. I know we have books lined on our shelves filed under the letter "R" for all things renewal. Perhaps you bought this book in hopes of understanding what it actually looks like to renew your mind; if that's the case, then good, because that's exactly what this is. However, not by your strength, but by God's.

I spent forty years in search of how I could renew my mind, renewing it through ways that I had devised. I had done my best to take scriptures and apply them to that which I wanted or needed. I had several Christian self-help books that I had attempted (and failed) to apply as a list of dos and don'ts. Their principles left me powerless to sin and kept me in the "sin, repent, forgive, repeat" cycle for far too long. I also had their trusted seven-step program for "getting over it" (whatever it may be). My efforts and energies produced very little, if any, progress in my life. But my time in the Word, along with the help of the trusted Holy Spirit, actually led to transformation, with new outlooks and perspectives that were actually true. It wasn't just a hopeful principle that someone had suggested I do, but spiritual truths that I just needed to play over and over in my mind in order to see them manifest in my life.

I warn you not to take that last sentence in the wrong way, as it's not some magic formula you can apply to see freedom. Without intimacy with God and the deep knowing of Jesus, these truths will still remain powerless. But a healthy balance of the Word and time spent alone with the Holy Spirit is what brought about results, not a self-driven, human formula that states, "If you just do this and believe this, you will be free."

No sir, you cannot be free on your own, even if you memorised the Bible front and back (as some scholars do). No, my friend, you must value and prioritise intimacy with God, as your relationship with Jesus is the entire reason God desires you to be free. Freedom allows you to know God unhindered, as there is nothing holding you back from His presence or love.

That's why replacing that broken record is so important, because those lies you're believing, that sin you're struggling with, is just a tactic of the enemy to keep you from God. Freedom is not for selfish gain; freedom is for you to know God completely and without hindrance.

There's also one more very important aspect to walking in freedom and allowing the Holy Spirit to transform your heart: obedience.

We can read all the diet books on the planet hoping and wishing to lose weight, but if we don't apply the food plans and exercise regimes, we will not be any further along than we were before we purchased the books (except a little poorer because of all the wasted money). And what about purchasing a treadmill for the bedroom, believing it's going to be the ultimate motivator for my strength, endurance, and weight loss for a 5K run that I dream of embarking on some day? If I have great intentions but have no follow-through, I will always, and I do mean always, come up short. Never succeeding. And the treadmill will be listed for sale and the diet books brought to a second-hand store.

I found this to be true in my Bible time. I began to read about what God desired of me and for me, but I needed to walk in obedience to all that He was asking of me. I began to see that intimacy with Him was necessary; essential. I needed to prioritise my time with the Lord, just as I had done when I first received the six-minute challenge. I needed to be obedient to the request to read the Word, as I knew somewhere deep down that God had requested it of me. Not because it was a religious task I needed to do to be accepted, but because He knew I needed truth and revelation in order to find freedom. I needed to obey the truth once it was revealed to me by replaying the scriptures in my mind, even though they didn't seem to be doing anything. I also needed to be obedient to the urge in my spirit to read my Word or pray, even when it was early in the morning or inconvenient, because that was when God was urging me to lean into Him.

It's true that God loved me unconditionally, yes, but my response to His love, my reply to it, and my receiving of the gift of His Son was only evident through my choice to follow in obedience as I continued to pursue Him. All that was required of me to begin the journey was to accept the free gift of Jesus's death and resurrection for my codeath and resurrection, and to walk in ever-increasing obedience and faith as truths were slowly revealed to me. It's not a 100-metre sprint; it's a marathon. It's slow and steady, gradually building as you remain intentional and obedient, not neglecting the value of the Word of God or the value of alone time with Jesus.

So how did I ultimately reach this renewing of the mind and put truth in its place in a practical way? Why, tea parties and moments at the waterfront. And if that doesn't work for you, then it's backyards and barbecues. Or if that still doesn't resonate with your more refined tastes, then how about jazz and Jesus? No matter the combination, Jesus will meet you there.

If you're still playing that broken record, and you're struggling with symptoms like anxiety, depression, self-loathing, a lack of joy, or bondage to addictions and sin, then take heart; your track change is coming. Jesus loves you so much that as you allow Him into your everyday life, His powerful love stories will do most of the work for you.

When I read the Word, I began to see, understand, and know

that the love of God (my form) was the foundational truth that I had needed all along to receive His promises. His love led me to believe that I truly was holy and blameless because of Jesus, that I truly was apart of a royal priesthood. I began to believe that I was indeed a partaker in the divine nature through the Holy Spirit when I was born again. These are things I would have questioned had I not understood that God's love for me was so radical that I really could be made completely new and free from sin.

You may still question these promises, even though they are clearly expressed in the Bible as true, and that's okay. Because the purpose of this book is to explain and hopefully inspire the process of receiving God's great and glorious freedoms. Understanding these spiritual truths God has given us leads to not only reading about freedom but experiencing it in our lives as we actually walk in (and, yes, dance in) the manifestations of God's goodness, things like being able to overcome temptation and say no to sin anytime a desire or temptation arises.

Things like believing you have the authority to pray and be heard by God, leading to miraculous healings, answered prayers, and salvations. Things like being able to go to God anywhere and at anytime without hindrances. It's one day finally feeling confident in God's great love for you and knowing that no matter what, He loves you and is for you.

It is finally feeling like you are valued, loved, and worthy of God's affections for you. It's not feeling depraved, wretched, wicked, or sinful; it's accepting the new creation God has made you, walking in it, and living from the new nature the Spirit has given you. When you allow God's love songs to play on repeat in your mind, I am confident that you will begin to believe them to be true, that you really are who He says you are.

Now that I have revealed to you in one of my own "Dawn-isms," a simple illustration of what it looks like to renew your mind, what record would you say you allow to play in your ears? Have you been listening to the devil and his orchestra of lies, guilt, and condemnation? Has he been singing a song of anxiety, anger, sadness, or gloom over you? Does the soundtrack feel dark and heavy? Or have you switched the track altogether by the great power of Jesus and begun singing praises to God for His sweet and uplifting melodies?

No matter where you are in experiencing Jesus's freedom and love, what He says about you is finished, completed, confirmed. Even now, let me exhort you with this last verse that leaves me cranking up God's Word in my mind on high.

> For the LORD your God is living among you. He is a mighty savior. He will take delight in you with gladness. With his love, he will calm all your fears. He will rejoice over you with joyful songs. (Zephaniah 3:17 NLT)

The Hebrew word for *rejoice* means to spin around under violent emotion, and the phrase "rejoice over you" means to dance, skip, leap, and spin in joy (Barb Smith, Opentheword.org).

Am I the only one who wants to get off of my chair and offer an impromptu praise fest? Are we getting the incredibleness of the actions of God in this verse? God, the very God of all the universe, is rejoicing over you. Have you ever considered the fact that God dances over you? It's no wonder I find myself dancing; my Father does.

Oh, this is your daily bread right here, folks. Fresh baked just for you. Fresh strawberry preserves, anyone? Breathe deeply the beautiful aroma it creates, and let it satisfy your soul.

Jesus, the One in whom we delight, the One who is our very life; we are who You say we are. Come on, let's declare that over us again: We are who You say we are, God. And again:

We are who you say we are, God.

Phew! Now that was a lot to digest, right? Let's take a moment and be grateful for our spiritual fat pants (LOL).

Seven

Who Do You Say I Am?

> I pray that your hearts will be flooded with light so that
> you can understand the confident hope he has given
> to those he called—His holy people who are his rich
> and glorious inheritance. (Ephesians 1:18 NLT)

Back before I ever understood God's love or His desire for intimacy, I was in a place where I also didn't understand my new identity in Jesus. Just as I explained in the previous chapter, due to my lack of knowledge, I naturally defaulted to believing that I was still the same person I was before I knew Jesus. I continued to allow the SKD album that had been playing since I was a child to drone on and on. I genuinely believed it was all I would ever know and all I ever deserved. I believed that Christ had saved me and forgiven me, and that said truths were all that had come from my relationship with Jesus. I only ever saw my repentance and baptism as professing my need and love for Jesus, but I never understood the reality of rebirth.

The term "born-again Christian" is not just a nice title we have as believers; it's a spiritual truth that happens when we receive Jesus as our Lord and surrender our very lives to Him. It says in the Bible that when we accept Jesus as Lord (not just simply believing in Him but giving Him control over our lives), we die to our old self and are born again. We were once dead in sin, our spirits destined for eternal death, just as our flesh is destined to die as well. But Jesus came to remove eternal death by bringing forth eternal life through His holy sacrifice: His death on the cross.

Many people understand that the sacrifice of Jesus led to the eternal forgiveness of sins; however, what many seem to miss is the literal spiritual rebirth that happens when we come to know Christ. If Jesus was only a sacrifice that led to the forgiveness of sins, then that would mean we are still under the slavery of sin, destined to sin forever.

If you believe this to be true, you may also say that we will be free from sin officially upon our earthly death, thus allowing us to be completely sin-free in our essence once we receive our eternal body. If you think this, you may also think that our flesh is inherently sinful and will forever cause us to sin, even after we become believers. The issue with this idea is that it leaves us in slavery to sin for the rest of our lives, thus resulting in that partial freedom narrative discussed earlier. It also causes us immense shame, guilt, and a continual separation from God, as we are in a continual state of sin awareness.

Our relationship with God will be focused more on avoiding sin than on spending time with Jesus, and if we *do* sin, we often feel we have to work our way back into God's acceptance. It's that cycle of sin, repent, forgive, and repeat: We sin, we repent (often with shame and guilt), we are forgiven by God, and eventually, we start the cycle again. This cycle is not what Christ died for; He died to set you free from sin so you would be made holy and righteous, fully capable through the power of the Holy Spirit to overcome this cycle and grow in ever-increasing intimacy with God.

You see, Jesus knew that sin is what kept you in a place where you couldn't fully commune with a Holy God. So to reconcile you to God and to restore a right relationship with Him, He had to make you holy, a compatible companion. Remember how I explained that we are the Bride of Christ? Do you think Jesus would want to marry someone who was unholy or unrighteous? Do you think God the Father would want His Son to marry someone who was wicked? It makes sense that a Holy God would desire a holy relationship with a holy bride, for He is "not a God who delights in wickedness; evil may not dwell with [Him]" (Psalm 5:4 ESV).

So if we are still sinners and in bondage to sin, then how can we also be the Bride of Christ? If we are still sinners, how can we also be holy, blameless, and righteous in God's sight?

Many people would argue that the term "in God's sight" would refer to a positional holiness and righteousness. They would argue that positionally, you are all of those things, but in your human reality, you are not. This is most certainly untrue and contradictory, as God cannot deem something as holy or righteous unless that very thing is holy and righteous. Remember, what God says is true, as "it [is] impossible for God to lie" (Hebrews 6:18 NLT).

So where does this term *positionally* stem from, as though God has on a pair of righteousness glasses that allow Him to overlook our seeming unrighteousness? Nowhere. The Bible never once speaks of a "positional" or "theoretical" or "once you die" holiness or righteousness. It never says that we become a new creation or find freedom from sin upon our physical death. The Bible is very clear that these things occur upon our spiritual death and our spiritual rebirth. This rebirth happens upon our acceptance of Jesus; we are cocrucified with Christ and coresurrected with Him in our spirits. For Paul states, in a present tense and not a past tense, that Christ lived in him in his physical body, for,

> My old self has been crucified with Christ. It is no longer I who live, but Christ lives in me. So I live in this earthly body by trusting in the Son of God, who loved me and gave himself for me. (Galatians 2:20 NLT)

Paul was not stating that he would die in the future and then Christ would dwell in him; it is clear that he already died and Christ was already living in him, following Paul's acceptance of Jesus. Jesus tells His disciples about the importance of their rebirth before their physical death: "I assure you, no one can enter the kingdom of God without being born of water and the Spirit. Humans can reproduce only human life, but the Holy Spirit gives birth to spiritual life. So don't be surprised when I say, 'You'd must be born again'" (John 3:5–7 NLT).

Jesus is clear that to inherit the kingdom of God (eternal life), you must be born again. Through revelation from the Holy Spirit, Paul teaches very clearly that this rebirth has already occurred upon our surrender to Jesus, as he states, "You have died with Christ, and he has set you free from the spiritual powers of this world" (Colossians 2:20 ESV).

> If anyone is in Christ, he is a new creation; old things have passed away, and look, new things have come. (2 Corinthians 5:17 ESV)

This "new creation" Paul is referring to here is the spiritual rebirth Jesus was explaining to His disciples. John also completely lays it out in his recount of Jesus's life by stating in John 1:12–13 (ESV), "But to all who believed him and accepted him, he gave the right to become children of God. They are reborn—not with a physical birth resulting from human passion or plan, but a birth that comes from God."

This now leads me back to my first point: God desired to give His Son in marriage to a Holy Bride. And how did He do that?

He created humans in His very likeness, a compatible companion; however, humans chose to go their own way and lost their God-given identity by enslaving themselves to sin. Although God's original intention for humankind was to be holy like God, they became sinful and lived contrary to the Lord's wishes. However, as I explained, God's intentions and purposes for us haven't changed; remember Jeremiah 29:11? He knew the plans He had for us even before Christ was revealed, because He knew that one day, we would be redeemed and be made to be like Him once again. And so, through the selfless and radical sacrifice of Jesus, God was able to create for Himself a holy people.

This leads me to my next point in addressing our new identities in Jesus: If you don't believe you were made holy by Jesus, you will forever try to become holy through works.

Much of the New Testament can become very legalistic if we don't understand that we have been given a new nature and a new identity. If we believe that Paul is telling us to do certain thing so that we will *become* holy, we will continue to sin, as we are still living under a "works mentality." Even though Jesus came so we wouldn't have to live under the control of the law anymore, if we believe we are still sinners, we will use what Paul has directed as a different kind of law.

The truth is, if you are living under any form of behaviour management or imposing any form of external rule, you are not living by the Spirit. For the Spirit doesn't impose anything as to burden you; the Spirit produces it from the inside out, causing you to live holy and righteous, just as Jesus is Holy and righteous. In other terms, some people see Paul's letters as rules to live by so that once you do so, *then* you become holy. As though you are only holy once you act and live holy. But the Bible doesn't say that you can become righteous or holy by the law (or *any* law, for that matter).

The Bible does say, "By his divine power, God has given us everything we need for living a godly life" (2 Peter 1:3 ESV).

In another version, "We have received all of this by coming to know him, the one who called us to himself by means of his marvelous glory and excellence. And because of his glory and excellence, he has given us great and precious promises. These are the promises that enable you to share his divine nature and escape the world's corruption caused by human desire" (2 Peter 1:3–4 ESV).

The Bible is clear that we are new creations, born of the Spirit, and free from sin. So what does this mean for us on this journey of renewing the mind?

This, my friends, is the main track on God's LMA record; if you only but heed, it will consequently lead to living a "Life More Abundant." If you have been listening to the lies of the devil's album that have stated you are unworthy, unholy, unrighteous, and wicked, this new way of living will surely give you a little hop in your step.

The devil has used those lies to keep you in shame and guilt. He wants you to believe that you are incompatible with God so that you continue to try and work your way to holiness, making you think you're unholy and sinful. He does that in two ways.

First, he keeps you in bondage to sin by making you believe you are in bondage to sin. This causes you to keep giving into temptation because you believe you don't have power over it. It also causes you to feel shameful because you know how God feels about sin; you know sin is wrong, but because you believe you are sinful, you feel you can never live up to God's standards.

Second, the devil keeps you in bondage to the law, even though it's not the same law that the Jews were under. He makes you believe that God only wants you if you are doing or acting the right way; this puts the burden on your performance and does not leave room for grace. This stems from believing that holiness is produced through living holy.

But put truth in its place: Jesus made you holy through His death. You are holy, so you will live holy. It is a transformation that happens from the inside out, not the outside in. This internal transformation of becoming holy happens in the heart, for "it's not what goes into your body that defiles you; you are defiled by what comes from your heart" (Mark 7:15 ESV).

Jesus is stating that nothing can make us unclean from the outside in, just as nothing can make us clean from the outside in. We are made unclean by what is in our hearts, not from what we do. What we do merely proves that our hearts are wicked or good. Because God knew that the sinful nature inside of us (that which made us slaves to sin) is what caused us to live sinfully. And because the law could only prove that we were sinful and not remove the sinful nature altogether, Jesus died so that we could be free from the sinful nature. "When you came to Christ, you were 'circumcised,' but not by a physical procedure. Christ performed a spiritual circumcision—the cutting away of your sinful nature" (Colossians 2:11 NLT).

Thanks be to God, who has freed us from that which once made us sinners and has now given us a new heart and a new spirit that is a partaker in the divine nature.

Grasping this biblical truth that you are no longer wicked, unholy, or unrighteous is imperative in walking in the freedom Jesus paid for. If you believe in any way that you are still the "old man," like I once did, and you allow the SKD record to play without ever putting truth in its place, you will never live the abundant life Jesus died for. You will either live as a sinner by faith, or you will live as a saint by faith in what Jesus truly accomplished for you on the cross.

Don't you see why it's so very important to be in your word and to spend time with Jesus? Since you put off the old self and its sinful nature by accepting Jesus, you must also put on the new nature; that is, the nature and character of Jesus. And how do you do this? You must first know Jesus to know your new nature.

If you never spent time with Jesus or spent time in your Word, how would you know the very nature of the Spirit living within you? How would you know when you were living in your new nature or when you were allowing the learned behaviours of your old nature to control you? There is no way to understand what it means to be a new creation if you don't understand Jesus and if you don't read your Word, again reiterating the importance of these practices. You must be in the Word. Jesus Himself resisted the devil's temptations through the power, authority, and use of the words of the Holy Scriptures.

God has given you complete access to His triple-platinum album that states you are loved, holy, righteous, and full of His Spirit; will you hit replay and go back to the same-old, same-old? It's your choice. My friends, you can't play for both teams, for once you know the truth about your freedom from sin, you can't choose to live in it any longer. You can no longer make excuses by stating, "That's just the way I am." You are who God says you are.

You can either accept His liberating truths and venture the path of understanding your new nature and what it looks like to live as such, or stay in the shackles Jesus already freed you from.

Hard pass, I know, but it is your choice to catch it and run the play.

Eight

Being Intentional: Being Deliberate and Purposed within Your Intentions

---

The effectiveness of the truth and the level of freedom you will experience all depend on your intentionality and active partnership with the Holy Spirit.

I want you to imagine a lion. Not the fictional, cuddly kind like the one on a toddler's bed; no, this one isn't in the mood to be friends. Imagine this lion is angry, and he's looking for something to devour or, moreso, some *one*. Let's turn the object of the lion's attention towards someone like you. His intentions and his instinct are not to protect you. He's going to do what is necessary to quench his hunger and feed his raging anger. His nature is to be intentional in his purposes: steal, kill, and destroy, no matter the cost. He will not listen to your cries for help. He will not be concerned about what this means to your family. His intentions are clear: kill. He is not concerned with your desires, either; he's made up his mind.

I'm not trying to instill fear with this image, but I want you to see the urgency of this chapter. We have an enemy, one who "prowls around like a roaring lion looking for someone to devour" (1 Peter 5:8 NLT). Previously, we read in Ephesians 6 that our enemy has a definitive game plan and a seemingly strong line-up. These are the teammates of our opposition. And their team? "Steal, Kill, Destroy." On the back of their jerseys, they proudly define themselves as "Principalities. Powers. Rulers of darkness. Spiritual wickedness." What a line-up, right? A self-proclaimed lion as their captain, a name like SKD, and players that have been known to rule this world: quite an intimidating team to be reckoned with. And their goal? Yep. You know this by now: Steal! Kill! Destroy!

Just like that lion whose vendetta is against you, true to his nature. He shows no concern for your well-being. He does not care about you, your family, your goals, your dreams. His only goal is to keep you as far away from God the Father as possible. By any means possible. This is his intention. He is deliberate. Purposeful. Intentional. Make no mistake: The only way to beat people as deliberate and intentional as the devil is to beat them at their own game.

Are you intentional in winning the game against the enemy? Or has he been throwing you around the court, parading his lion-like stature and full-pressing you with his wicked line-up? Not to worry; you've come to the right place.

This momma has seen the enemy lose time and time again, and she's ready to train you in victory, just as the Holy Spirit has trained her.

As we continue to unpack these spiritual truths about our identity and our relationship with God, we must also be intentional with what we've learned. The effectiveness of the truth and the level of freedom you will experience all depend on your intentionality and active partnership with the Holy Spirit. Just as the enemy made it easy for you to believe lies, so the Holy Spirit will make it easier for

Putting Truth in Its Place

you to believe the truth. And just as the enemy faithfully whispered lies in your ears, so will the Holy Spirit faithfully whisper truths; it's up to you as to which one you listen to. Believe it or not, you actually decide whose word you believe.

Like Adam and Eve, from birth we have an inherent tendency to listen to the voice of Satan. But now, us being alive in Christ and dead to the old man, the Spirit inside of us has an inclination to listen to the voice of truth. Our job in the matter is to know said truths, so that when we are faced with a thought, we are able to discern what is from God (truth) and what is from Satan (lies).

Although the old nature loved to listen to Satan, I want to reassure you that even if you do struggle with lies, the new heart God has placed inside of you truly does long to believe the truth. All we have to do is partner with the process and allow God to strengthen us as we recite His Word in our minds. All it takes is getting that which is written on the tablet of our hearts (the truth of God) to be the record we play in our minds.

Many of us actually allow the enemy to infiltrate our thought realm, thus controlling our lives, because we have forgotten we even have an enemy. I'm not sure what you expected from the devil, but he is still as sly as he was in the garden of Eden. He has been slithering around deceitfully (emphasis on *deceitful*), seeking whom he may devour, both believer and unbeliever alike. Just take a look at our world; I am certain we can all agree that we are surrounded by evil. It seems as though our world, especially as of late, has become saturated with every kind of evil. As believers, we know that this rise of the enemy's power is the result of our society removing Jesus from schools, workplaces, homes, and even some churches. The enemy has taken these opportunities to attack and cause great destruction. It's almost as though we have come to hear the enemy's roar as a soft purr, nonthreatening. Or better yet, we have completely forgotten that he is our enemy at all. Both of these scenarios have set our world on a screaming spiral course into destruction, fulfilling one of the enemy's game plans.

The only One with power to overcome the enemy is Jesus. If we as believers are not living as Jesus lived and believing the truth that He spoke over us, we remain powerless to the devil. In all honesty, believers have given the devil permission to enter said spaces of our society because we have not upheld the truth. For if we upheld and lived out the truth, we would know that we have all authority over the devil: over all his lies, schemes, and accusations. Jesus quite literally says to His disciples, "Look, I have given you authority over all the power of the enemy, and you can walk among snakes and scorpions and crush them. Nothing will injure you" (Luke 10:19 NLT).

The Bible also says,

> For though we live in the world, we do not wage war as the world does. The weapons we fight with are not the weapons of the world. On the contrary, they have divine power to demolish strongholds. We demolish arguments and every pretension that sets itself up against the knowledge of God, and we take captive every thought to make it obedient to Christ. (2 Corinthians 10:3–5 NLT)

We are guaranteed this victory, but it doesn't come through physical defence or with weapons. It is a battle in our minds, a battle in our thought realm; it's quite simply a battle against lies. The Bible says, "Stay alert! Watch out for your great enemy, the devil. He prowls around like a roaring lion, looking for someone to devour" (1 Peter 5:8 NLT).

Not to devour physically, for few of us can say we've had physical experiences with the devil and his army. No, this is another kind of devouring, something spiritual.

Putting Truth in Its Place

The truth is, the devil is roaring lies. He is roaring deception. He is the great deceiver. His only power against you, his strongholds in your life, all pertain to the arguments and pretenses that set themselves up against the knowledge of God. In simpler terms, the devil uses cunning lies to trap you into believing them. By believing his lies, he keeps you in bondage and ultimately controls the way you live. It is the foundation of what we believe that ultimately rules our life, and if we believe lies that say we are guilty, unworthy, unloved, and full of shame, we will live condemned and imprisoned. For God was never speaking of a physical freedom when He spoke of setting the captives free, for we all know that Paul was imprisoned many times, even post-Christ. But God was always speaking of freedom from the bondage of sin and the bondage of lies (something we will touch on more in later chapters).

So what does the Word say we should do?

Take every thought captive, and make them obedient to Christ. (2 Corinthians 10:5 NIV)

This, my friends, in a spiritual nutshell, is the renewing of the mind.

It is the imperative process of assessing our beliefs, filtering them through the truth of the Word, and throwing out all the junk and lies that do not align with what God says about us or our lives. This process takes time and intentionality.

Let's start by revisiting the definition of intentionality: being deliberate and purposed with or in your intentions. In order for us to make our thoughts obedient to Christ, we must be intentional. We must be purposed. Deliberate. Webster defines the word *intention* as "What one intends to do or bring about, to direct the mind on." Being intentional is to direct the mind; to actively put our thoughts somewhere and not just allow them to run rampant.

Within this frame of reference, let me ask you a few questions: What is it that you intentionally think about? Are you even intentional with your thoughts? What is it that you allow to dictate how you view your life? Why is it that you think the way you do, and what is it that empowers you to think in such a way?

If we aren't careful or intentional, our thought realm can easily be overtaken by lies, which ultimately results in bondage. If we don't assess our beliefs and determine why we think the way we do, we will continue to live as though we are defeated, unworthy, full of anxiety and depression, and worst of all: in a continual cycle of sin. We may also allow our emotions and our experiences to dictate our thoughts because we feel a certain way, instead of believing the truth over our emotions.

I often used to think my emotions were the end-all and be-all; how I felt screamed louder than anything anyone could tell me. But the truth is, your emotions come from Adam, and as a new creation, you have to learn to bring your emotions under submission to the Spirit and the truth, much like your thoughts. To put it simply, as there are numerous truths in the Bible that we have yet to learn; it is the process of taking your eyes off of lies and looking instead to Jesus. For the Word says that in Jesus, all of God's promises for us are Yes and Amen, meaning that everything God has for us is hidden in the life of Jesus, who is, again, our very life.

Colossians 3:2 (NIV) says, "Set your minds on things above, not on earthly things!" Sounds pretty intentional, don't you think? Doesn't leave much room for other things, nor does it give you permission to think about anything other than Jesus. It's not a "could you." It's not an "if you feel like it"; it's not an option at all. The Bible states very clearly that we are to "set" our minds. Sounds pretty concrete, don't ya think? It's where our eyes are fixed and focused without distraction, given to Jesus and the truth of who He is.

It is not eyes taken by a "lust of the eyes or flesh," as 1 John 2:16 (NIV) says, "for everything in the world—the lust of the flesh, the lust of the eyes, and the pride of life—comes not from the Father but from the world." If our eyes are on anything but Jesus, we can easily fall into the trap of the other team, where the devil comes to steal, kill, and destroy. We can even get to a place where we believe the devil's lies so strongly that we begin to defend said lies.

Ouch.

Have you been letting team SKD intimidate you? Have you felt powerless to their attack? Have you been so focused on their lies that you have missed God's offensive truths laid out in the Word? You can be so oblivious to or unintentional with the enemy that you get to a place in your life where you actually bench yourself. You are on neither the offensive nor the defensive, but you willingly, without realising it, leave your side of the court wide open. It's like you have given him an open space to literally walk right in and score endless points on your basket. And he isn't even trying. In your mind, he has made you believe you aren't even good enough to play him. He has used you against yourself. Because, my beloved, the devil knows you play for the best team in the league.

And what team is that? LMA. And who's the coach of that team? The Father. And who's the captain? Jesus. And who are the supporting teammates? Why, the body of Christ. All in complete unity through the power of the Holy Spirit, equipped with game plans the devil himself has never even seen before.

But there you sit, benched. All because you think you can't play. Just like the way you thought you had a hole in your bucket.

Come on, teammate; it's time to get yourself up off that bench and get fired up to play. The team needs you; I need you. No more watching the enemy score, thinking he has the victory in the bag. No sirree, my friend; he has a valiant opponent who is ready to crush him.

Oh, dear one, let me reassure you that God does not want any of us to stay on the bench; that is not His original game plan for you. Jesus came so that we could be traded, at the highest price, to His team. We are not benched. We are not directed to run more laps, do more burpies, or shoot countless baskets; just because.

In our receiving and accepting of Jesus as Lord of our lives, we don't have to work our way onto the team; we are simply handed a jersey. We are declared a team member, a valued one. In fact, there are no second-strings, assistant captains, or hot shots on His team; we are all called into His family as beloved and adored.

Imagine, if you will, the crowd cheering as His team enters the stadium. The announcer broadcasts each name, introducing each one with excitement. "Presenting team LMA!" Today's line-up? Their jerseys stamped, not on the back, but boldly pressed on the front: "LOVED!" "BELOVED!" "ADORED!" "FORGIVEN!" "REDEEMED!" "RIGHTEOUS!" "HOLY!"

The crowd's applause is deafening; their angelic chorus resonating throughout heaven's halls. But wait; there's more. The announcer clears his throat and asks for quiet from the crowd so he can introduce the team captain. "Ladies and gentleman, may I please have your attention? I would like to introduce to you the Author of our faith, the Holy One, the Alpha and the Omega: Jesus!" The crowd roars with abundant praise and foolish dancing. I must admit that sitting still at the moment is a challenge, for I long to join the heavenly chorus as you receive your jersey and suit up. Come on, teammate. I see your jersey, and it is glorious.

This, my friends, is the journey from pain to healing, where we come into the understanding of our truths in Jesus. We are not to partake in any part of what the world has to offer, including the devil's lies. We are to have our eyes fixed on Jesus.

This simple illustration of a basketball game with opposing teams is to teach you the value of your place on God's team. It's to teach you that we do indeed have an enemy, one that merely roars like a lion. The fact is, he isn't even a lion. All he does is roar lies, and often very loudly. But once we allow the Holy Spirit to teach us the truth, to enable us with His divine power to see the truth, and to reveal the person of Jesus to our hearts, we become unstoppable.

We learn the enemy's plays, for he has been using the same ones since the garden. We learn our authority and our pivotal role on God's team. And we learn to stay close to the Captain, to the One who designed all of God's plays, the One who chose us to be on

His team in the first place, the One who teaches us and effortlessly moulds us into His Own image.

He longs to work with you, to train you, to teach you, to support you. So much so that He died for you. He knows His authority over the enemy; do you? Maybe you aren't even sure what team you're on, but worry not.

I once was like some of you are, caught between teams, not knowing which I stood for. So how did I get traded? Repentance! Brokenness! Surrender! Acceptance! And understanding!

Are you up for the trade? The price has already been paid, and your jersey awaits.

Nine

Repentance

This, repentance, is the process of saying yes to God, accepting His jersey, and then renewing your mind to believe that everything this jersey represents is who you have become.

It may seem odd to have a chapter on repentance right after the explanation and disclosure of our new nature in Christ, right? It would almost seem unnecessary, as this book is obviously geared towards those who profess to know Jesus. But let me continue on as to why this chapter is in fact necessary by metaphorically taking us courtside to a basketball game.

At this ball game, we can see team LMA lined up for the national anthem. They are focused, prepared, and full of adrenaline. Unlike the rest of the cheering crowd, thrilled to witness this all-star team about to play, you sit in a state of void. The crowd continues to cheer with excitement as the teams advance to their benches, prepared and ready for the game ahead. They know their positions, as they have practiced thoroughly. The gym rocks with the crowd's deafening cheers, but there you sit; still. You seem neither excited nor intrigued by the thrilling game taking place before your very eyes.

Your haze is interrupted by the referee who asks, "Aren't you playing today?" It takes a moment or two for the air to clear and you reply with a, "Sorry, are you talking to me?" He and the entire LMA team begin to call you to the court, to their bench. You stagger over in a state of misunderstanding and incomprehension.

The Coach hands you a jersey and asks, "Are you ready to play?"

God has been calling all of us back to Himself and to His team since the garden. He has revealed His heart to us time and time again through the scriptures and in the gentle calls of the Holy Spirit. He has forever been calling us back to the court. However, in our selfishness, we have chosen to sit on the sidelines. We choose to play for neither the devil (SKD) nor God (LMA). We have been satisfied neither cheering for nor participating with either team. We assume that our lack of decisiveness and complacency is just another area where God's grace abounds over us. We believe as though God is okay with us playing neither for nor against Him, that He is fine with our unassuming stance. We may even believe that this is where God's grace extends, as though our indecision and lack of passionate pursuit is outweighed by God's grace to receive us anyways. But does a groom desire a bride who isn't passionately in love with him?

Just as Jesus explains in the Gospel of Matthew, "Anyone who isn't with me opposes me, and anyone who isn't working with me is actually working against me" (Matthew 12:30 NLT). By choosing to sit on the sidelines, we are deemed as lukewarm, which Jesus responds to very clearly in the book of Revelation by saying, "I know all the things you do, that you are neither hot nor cold. I wish that you were one or the other! But since you are like lukewarm water, neither hot nor cold, I will spit you out of my mouth!" (Revelation 3:15–16 NLT).

The interesting thing with this illustration is the fact that the sidelines are owned by the devil and his team. Jesus stated in that verse from Matthew that if you aren't actively working with Him (playing for His team), you are, in fact, working against Him. And who is that opposing team? You guessed it: team SKD. If upon hearing this you are struck with conviction because you realise that you have been camping on the sideline, again I say, take heart. The purpose of this chapter is not only to inspire conviction, but also to inspire you to change.

While we are still alive on this earth, it is never too late to join God's team and fight the good fight, to know Jesus and to bring others into the right relationship with Him. It takes only a moment to renounce your old ways, to thank God for His unwavering forgiveness, and to accept His open invitation to join His team unhindered, just as He designed you! The truth is, upon receiving Jesus as the Lord of your life, you were given the jersey of team LMA right away. You were deemed fit and worthy to play alongside the best of the best, to play alongside Jesus. You were given a new identity that transformed you into the ultimate basketball star through the power of the Holy Ghost; of course, this is merely a figurative statement used to express your eligibility and supernatural ability to live the life God has called you to live.

Upon experiencing the powerful conviction of the Spirit to get off the sidelines and choose, what does God require of you in order to play alongside His all-star team?

Repentance.

Repentance simply looks like decisively leaving the sidelines and running towards God's team. It looks like receiving God's forgiveness upon the confession of your lukewarm state and embracing God's mercy and grace, which allows you to instantly join the team you were destined for. Repentance is not something we use *when* we sin or live contrary to God, but *if* we do such things. It is not a continual process that fits nicely into that cycle of sin, repent, forgive, repeat; to repent is to stop what you were once doing and live the way God has enabled you to.

In the Bible, the word *repentance* is *metanoia,* which is defined as a summons to a personal, absolute, and ultimate unconditional surrender to God as Sovereign. Though it includes sorrow and regret, it is much more than that. In repenting, one makes a complete change of direction toward God. Repentance means to accept that you can't do it on your own and to receive the enabling grace of the

Holy Spirit to empower you to live a godly life. You partner with the Holy Spirit to walk in constant fellowship with Jesus, and to say no to your old ways of living. Repentance happens when we denounce the way we were doing something and choose to go God's way. You don't need to spend an hour of weeping and apologising, hoping God will forgive you. Repentance looks like accepting the conviction of your heart even if it's painful, asking for God's forgiveness (or even just thanking Him, as we know He forgives us already), and then saying no to sulking in shame and guilt because you are already forgiven.

God has already thrown your old lukewarm ways into the sea of forgetfulness, and He will honor your surrender and clothe you with righteousness and holiness, just as He promised to do through Christ. The jersey He has given you is meant to become your second skin, as some would say, as something we wear, not something we merely hold in our hand as a token of God's love. That powerful LMA jersey is our new identity, and with it comes power, authority, and the fruit of the Spirit. But much like the LMA record in our minds, we must also put on this jersey daily. We must remember which team God has called us to and remember that we have been given the eternal privilege to wear His logo.

If we aren't intentional in believing that we are forgiven, accepted, and clothed by God's righteousness, we can easily listen to that SKD record and believe we are no different than before. We must put on God's jersey always, remembering what it means to be a part of His team. We must remember that said jersey actually clothes us in the righteousness of God. That jersey states we are loved, worthy, valuable, holy, and righteous. It also gives us full authority over the opposing team, team SKD. You've decided to accept His request to join and to unashamedly wear His team's jersey, no longer on the sidelines. You're now on team LMA.

You haven't played with them before, but you can feel adrenaline pumping through your body and an innate understanding of what you're capable of doing. Although you've never dunked before, nor would it have been physically possible even if you had wanted to, this time, you just know you can do it. You know you can dribble, pass, weave, swerve, and yes, dunk. God looks at you this time and asks if you're ready to play.

If you're like me, you're wondering why a Coach of such caliber would put one so green into the game so quickly. We would assume that any new converts or rookies would be too inexperienced to play on the court right away. But to this Coach, you aren't made ready over time; you become ready by accepting His invitation to indwell within you. The Coach's game plan was set in motion in the beginning, and His plans and purposes for each team member were already designed and prepared. What is required of us is simply accepting it, walking in it, and living out His righteousness in us, as though we are indeed righteous. It's saying yes to God and putting on the jersey that is the nature of Christ within us and putting off the old man.

> Put off our old self, which belongs to your former manner of life and is corrupt through deceitful desires, and to be renewed in the spirit of your minds, and to put on the new self, created after the likeness of God in true righteousness and holiness. (Ephesians 4:22–24 ESV)

This is the process of saying yes to God, accepting His jersey, and then renewing your mind to believe that everything this jersey represents is who you have become. So what has happened within the time you chose to leave your old ways and accepted God's invitation? By you accepting His request to join the team, you responded in obedience by walking intentionally toward God. Although you had nothing to offer Him in skill or ability, He took your obedience and intentionality as a go-ahead to enabling you with His Spirit. He was never looking for the most skilled or qualified player, He was always looking for His beloved child to receive His invitation to join Him so He could reveal His own power through you. He didn't just want you to join the team; He wanted to transform you into a valuable team member who represents Him well. It wasn't anything you could have done that deemed you worthy, for He knew that once you intentionally repented and obeyed, you would be exactly who you were called to be.

I hope in this moment, your heart is yearning for the jersey God has for you, because it's readily available right now. By you responding the way I've explained here, you are revealing the intentions of your heart to the Lord. You are showing Him that you are no longer content to sit courtside. You are showing Him that although you may still have unbelief, you want to believe that He can completely transform you, and you desire to start by simply saying yes to His invitation. Once you do this, and as you continue to read the Word and seek the Lord with your whole heart, you will no longer question your identity or wonder which jersey you should wear.

You will begin to see the transformation I am speaking of; you will begin to see how God truly will work through you by the power of His Holy Spirit.

You will begin to naturally have the inclination to dunk (in a literal sense, you will naturally begin to say no to sin, to desire goodness and love, and to live more selflessly). You won't have to question whether you are on the team or not, because once you receive His invitation by faith and begin to believe that what He says about you is true, you will begin to experience a heart like God's. You will powerfully trample over the enemy. You will be able to resist the devil and his temptations. You will love radically and without restraint. Galatians 5:24 (NIV) says that "those who belong to Christ Jesus have crucified the flesh with its passions and desires." No longer will you play by the rules of the flesh, and no longer will you be held by that which draws and entices, for those who are fully clothed in righteousness will walk in the fruit of the Spirit.

Love, joy, peace, patience, kindness, goodness, faithfulness, gentleness, and self-control. (Galatians 5:22–23 ESV)

All of these are interwoven with God's powerful game plan that you now get to partake in. All because you chose to walk away from the sidelines and receive the God-given position you were born for.

Ten

Change

The beautiful thing about the kind of change God has for us, is that it is nothing we need to fear.

What Will Change?

Yep. An entire chapter dedicated to the most constant thing in our lives: change. You're probably hoping that this chapter is just a page or two at best, or that it will require very little effort and even less commitment. I'm sorry (but not really) to say that none of the above expectations are true about this section of our journey.

The word *change* can send most us into a physical and emotional conundrum, causing our blood pressure to elevate. It may even cause you to sweat in the most unlikely of places; yay! Perhaps you have struggled with something for so long that you actually believe it's impossible for you to change. Maybe you don't think it's possible for anyone to change because your life experiences have proven that to be true. Or maybe the thought of changing causes anxiety and pressure because you believe it to be associated with legalism or a works mentality.

Let me reassure you that no one is forcing you to do anything you don't want to do. Only you can allow God to transform you, and only you can decide how much. You have the choice to invite God into your heart and your life to allow Him Lordship, and you have the choice to obey Him once He begins revealing things to you.

Although this action of changing, or in better terms, being transformed, is done by the Spirit, you still have a pivotal role to play in allowing God to do the work He desires to.

Let me reassure you that change in your life is most certainly possible, and it does not require stress or the need to fear what is changing. It can be an empowering and uplifting journey that leads to greater strength in the Lord, not continual condemnation, shame, or guilt.

It's an easy burden, and the yoke is light; it's partnership with the Holy Spirit, and it's most certainly not equal. In fact, the Holy Spirit carries far more of the load than you ever will; however, He still invites you to be part of the process. Remember, your works do not make you holy; you are made holy so you live holy. And who makes you holy? The Holy Spirit.

If you, my dear friend, are already in a relationship with Jesus and have already accepted Him as your Lord, you have already experienced change. How do I know this for certain? You're reading this book. Why else would you spend hours of your life listening to some lady you don't know blabber on about putting truth in its place? And what do I know? All I can share with you is what I have learned from the Holy Spirit. You clearly thought it worthwhile to allow someone like me to teach you something valuable that God has revealed to me, proving that your intentions here are to know more about the Lord and your life as a believer. That in itself is change, because only those who have heard the call of the Lord will respond by purchasing a book that could lead them into deeper intimacy with God.

But there is more change to come as you continue to put truth in its place and believe all that God has for you in His precious promises, things we've discussed, like Life More Abundant, intimacy with God, freedom from sin and bondage, and a new identity in

Putting Truth in Its Place

Jesus. These promises we have unpacked are all things you will begin to experience in your life as you give up control and allow the truth to define you.

Just as we addressed the need for intentionality and obedience, we must also address giving up control. When we feel the need to control things, the idea of change can cause a lot of fear. Either we are afraid of change because we are afraid of losing control, or we are afraid that we cannot change the way we desire, thus leaving us feeling hopeless and destined to stay the same. The beautiful thing about the kind of change God has for us is that it's nothing we need to fear. We need not fear the way we will change, as in what we will become, and we need not fear how we will change. God is clear in His Word that He will transform us into the image of His Son and that He will do it through the mighty working power of His Spirit.

Paul is clear that God is the One who changes us when he writes to the Philippians, stating, "And I am certain that God, who began the good work within you, will continue his work until it is finally finished on the day when Christ Jesus returns" (Philippians 1:6 NLT).

> What a beautiful thing to allow God to create us into the masterpiece He destined us to be.
>
> For we are God's masterpiece. He has created us anew in Christ Jesus, so we can do the good things he planned for us long ago. (Ephesians 2:10 NLT)

I can assure you that although change in the Spirit is immediate, the external process of experiencing that change can take time. I have had my fair share of change myself; so much so that I could write a full series of encyclopedias on the subject.

I've had natural life changes, such as my father's heart attack, my own reconstructive surgery, a *Walking Dead*-category nervous breakdown, our beloved daughter attempting suicide and being admitted to the psych ward, learning that my daughter was living with and dating a girl, selling our home while my husband started Bible college when he was nearly fifty years old, and leaving jobs, family, and the city we called home for so long. Even beyond all of that, after we relocated to attend college, we had to move two more times, make new friendships, find a new church, start a new job, and all of this in a city we knew nothing about. I myself had attended this same Bible college, but that was twenty-eight years prior. And now here I am, revealing the accumulation of it all in this book.

In all honesty, writing this book feels a lot less daunting than what we've already journeyed. Praise God for His never-failing, never-ending faithfulness. I can promise you that there are many more events that have taken place, but I trust that you can identify with some of them. We have walked many a mile, wearing out some of the shoes along the way. I do know that my most beloved pair bear the designer label, Hope and Faith.

I trust you can appreciate that I do not speak into any of these things within the book through ignorance, for there are many things I understand and have compassion for. I know that you, my dear readers, have journeyed many a mile yourself; some even more than devastating than what we've experienced; some wearing out many pairs of shoes.

So how is it that we have journeyed (and, in many ways, are still journeying) these wild life changes without losing our minds? How on earth are we not wrought with despair, desperation, and depression? It's all because I experienced the most glorious changes yet: the changes that came from knowing Jesus and being known by Him. All because I embarked on that six-minute challenge to read my Word and spend time with the Lord. I myself have journeyed the renewing of the mind, putting truth in its place, receiving God's love for me, growing in intimacy, and learning my identity in Christ, and I am still changing. I stand here knowing that I am loved, free, and a brand-new creation, all because I allowed the Holy Spirit to change me, and here I am changed. But is it over? Oh, no; far from it. For I will continue to experience change until the day I die, or until Christ comes back to make me His bride, whichever comes first. I am beyond thankful that I allowed the truth of God's Word to penetrate my heart and my mind, to ultimately bring me into a place of unwavering faith that I am who God says I am. I have seen great changes in my behaviour, speech, and mindset, through my agreement and obedience to the Word of God. I have seen the character of Jesus being expressed through my very life; I have even seen victory time and time again over temptation and sin. But yet, I still have not arrived; change is still to come, for there is more to be revealed about Jesus and more to be revealed in me. So am I satisfied? Yes (well, for the moment, anyway).

At what point in my journey did I finally find myself satisfied with my walk with God? It all depends on how you define the word *satisfied*. I am deeply satisfied with the love of Jesus and the way I get to spend time with Him daily. I am also satisfied with my ever-changing life, as I know God is with me through it all. But am I satisfied as to say that I am complete, or that I have had enough? Absolutely not.

Even after five years on this journey, I still don't feel that sense of having arrived or being completely satisfied, for more is yet to come. There is more to know about Jesus, more to learn, more to experience, and more freedom to attain as I understand my identity even more. Having removed the veil of lies and dead thoughts, I eagerly await the glory that is to be revealed in me more and more, as I know my Creator.

> And we all, with unveiled face, beholding the glory of the Lord, are being transformed into the same image from one degree of glory to another. For this comes from the Lord who is the Spirit. (2 Corinthians 3:18 ESV)

What a beautiful verse. What a glorious truth. God has promised that as we behold the glory of the Lord with our unveiled faces, we will be transformed into that same image from glory to glory. This is exactly the purpose of this book and exactly the beauty of change.

> "For I know the plans I have for you," declares the LORD, "plans to prosper you and not to harm you, plans to give you hope and a future." (Jeremiah 29:11 NIV)

I can assure you that any changes God brings about in your life, whether you view them as good or bad, will lead to a hopeful future. Any changes you experience are designed for a purpose: His purpose. Our ultimate goal in life is to have greater intimacy with Jesus, and in my eyes, anything that can bring us into deeper understanding of Him is a blessing. No matter the changes, the experiences, or the challenges, God's plans for me are always good, and I can always count on Him to sustain me. For God's ways are immeasurably greater than I can think, dream, or imagine.

What Has Not Changed

Up until now, we have spoken so much of what has changed and not about what has stayed the same. Although change is good (great, even), having something we can rely on, something steady, that firm foundation in our lives is necessary to support all that change.

That, my friends, is Jesus.

Like I've explained all throughout this book, the truth about you and about God has not changed since the beginning. No sirree; it has been the same since before Adam and Eve were formed in the garden. Jesus was always destined to die, and you were always destined to be a child of God. You have always been loved by Jesus, and you will always be loved by Jesus.

The Spirit of God will always transform you into the image of your Creator, if you allow Him to, and the Spirit of God will always reveal Jesus to you. God always has good plans for you, and God always desires to be known by you. What God says about you has always been true, and what the devil says about you will always be a lie.

Team LMA has always had a spot available for you, and you will always have the choice to receive God's invitation, up until the day you die. God will always invite you to come and grow in intimacy with Him, and He will always enable you to come into His presence with confidence and boldness. Christ will always desire you to be His Bride, and He will always fight to remove the veil from your precious eyes.

You may change. Life may change. Your very foundation may change after reading this book. But what will *never* change is the love of your beloved Groom and the intentions He has for you.

I pray the veil is lifted, you change the record album, and you proudly wear the team jersey that professes "LMA." I pray you feel strengthened and encouraged by the Spirit to embark on your own six-minute journey and learn the truth about who you are in Jesus. May you be bold and courageous in your pursuit of change and receptive as the Holy Spirit works in you.

Eleven

Challenge Accepted?

May you receive the blossoming hope that there is more for you in Jesus.

After having expressed my very heart to you on the subject of freedom and intimacy with Jesus, I believe you are now in a place to receive the same challenge I was once offered; we have now come to the point where there is work for you to do. It is time for you to begin your own six minutes and tea parties (if you haven't already begun). If you have come this far in your readings, it likely means you are indeed ready to receive that which I am offering to you, with the help of the Holy Spirit. At this point, you may even be wondering how you ever believed there was such thing as partial freedom. Maybe you have been living in this partial freedom narrative your entire Christian life and just now are realising there may be more.

Maybe you have been genuinely devoted to Jesus for years, with a sincere love for Him, but were simply taught wrong by those you trusted. Maybe you're the one who taught people that the partial freedom narrative was true, but maybe you yourself never knew that it wasn't. Take heart, because God knows your sincerity of heart, and He delights when any of His children come to understand their true identity and inheritance in Christ; there is no shame or condemnation.

Some of you may not have known these things because you simply haven't opened your Bible to find the truth for yourself. Or maybe you lack intimacy with Jesus, so you never really had the opportunity to learn the truth. All this to say, don't worry about the past or how it was that you got to this place, but certainly don't ignore that which He is revealing to you now.

God delights in the truth, and He delights in your freedom; receive His invitation, and humbly receive His correction, as He reveals lies that may have been inhibiting you for years. Remember, His love for you has never changed, no matter the circumstance you find yourself in. Your responsibility now is to respond to the truth and to actively expose the lies that God reveals to you. For the Word of God says,

> If anyone, then, knows the good they ought to do
> and doesn't do it, it is sin for them. (James 4:17 NIV)

This is especially true when dealing with sin in your life, as you can no longer say, "It's my human nature to sin." This verse also applies to intimacy with Jesus, as it is God's loving request for you to know Him, and if you neglect such an invitation while you live on this earth, why would you then receive eternal life, which is knowing God? Don't be deceived, for God is clear that those who do not know Him will be spit out of His mouth, no matter the gifts they walked in.

This is not to scare you by any means, but it is to inspire the sober judgement of your life to see where it is that you stand with God in this very moment.

Do you know Him? Are you still living in sin? Are you living in bondage?

I am believing that there is a part of you that has been awakened to the knowledge of complete freedom in Christ and to the love of God, who desires deeper intimacy with you. I pray you have received the hope God is inviting you into through the revelations of this book and through that which He has expressed in His Word. I pray you have a greater hunger to know Jesus and to discover all the promises He has fulfilled in you through His triumphant resurrection from the dead. And if you receive nothing else from this book other than a blossoming hope that there is more for you in Jesus, then this book has fulfilled its purpose. For we can no longer believe the lie that there is no hope for those who are experiencing partial freedom in their Christian life.

I personally know people, myself included, who have indeed experienced complete freedom in Jesus and are walking in intimacy they never knew was possible. They are free. Free. No longer enslaved by the throes and power of sin. No longer gripped and held captive by the clenches of despair, shame, guilt. No longer kept, restricted, trapped, and held in the prisons of destructive mindsets. But free. Completely free. Living a victorious life over sin and the throes of the enemy's lies and deceptions through the incredible power of the Holy Spirit and the unchanging powerful Word of God. Living victoriously. Living free. Dancing. Living in and understanding the life abundant that Jesus promised for us. All of this, my friends, is for you as well. Jesus promised this for all.

I now declare over you, hope. Jesus, our Blessed Hope.

I pray you continue to replay this truth, and the more than fifty scripture verses cited in this book, over and over in your mind until it becomes natural; until it becomes your very way of thinking. Renew your mind. Be intentional. Be purposed.

For the world, and even the church, may tell you that there is no hope, that we are doomed and will always be caught in a spiritual spin cycle, tossed and thrown around by that which the world believes to be true. But as I have clearly laid out in the pages of this book, we have the authority to change the track playing in our minds and to receive that which God has prepared for us. Although I have deeply loved sharing my heart and my understanding with you, I must now conclude my thoughts with a challenge.

Are you ready to be free from the agony of feeling trapped on a daily basis, whether it be from sin, mental illness, or any other kind of emotional bondage? Are you even just a little excited to hear that the partial freedom narrative you have been believing does not have to stay the same? Doesn't it excite you to know that not all of the thoughts in your mind are true and that you have the authority to control them? You control your thoughts; they don't control you.

Be encouraged today, dear ones. It is now time for you to pursue Jesus and to experience your own personal intimacy with your beloved God. It is time for you to learn the truth that God has spoken over you and the promises He has fulfilled with His Son, Jesus. It is time for you to read your Word with intentionality and begin to pursue the freedom God has called you to through your adoption as His child. No longer letting every thought and opinion define you, but you will learn to take your thoughts captive and begin to put truth in its place.

It is time for you to become intentional with your life, to become intentional with Jesus. As believers, we don't just get by, for we are called to thrive. We are not called to live a life less abundant, but more abundant. You can no longer stay in the old way of thinking once you have been awakened to the truth that Jesus wants more for you than to simply sit on the sidelines and watch; we both know this is not the salvation Jesus died for.

It is time for you throw off the old man and receive the revelations God gives to you concerning the new man; it is your responsibility to allow the Spirit to work through you as you begin to understand your new nature. Sin can no longer be your master, and lies can no longer be your excuse for living in sin or bondage. Although it is a process of understanding Jesus, His Word, and His Promises, it must begin somewhere. As you embark on this journey, I know that you will not be disappointed with the new adventures God has for you, as there are many that await.

From the moment you choose to receive and believe that God loves you, that He is singing over you, and that He gave so sacrificially

Putting Truth in Its Place

for you, you will actively begin to see all that was purposed, given, and accomplished, for you.

Oh, it's not anything to do with what I can offer you, aside from personal insight and some teachings within this book. Nor will you see transformation through a simple step-by-step plan that I will outline for you. All that you desire to see transformed in your life, whether that be freedom from sin or growing in intimacy with Jesus, will come to pass by surrendering to the power of the Holy Spirit and having a willing heart. Through the Word of God and because of your willingness to walk in obedience to the truths that will be illuminated to your heart, you will undoubtedly see transformation.

Hebrews 4:12 says the word of God is "alive." How could we ever partake in something that is alive and come away feeling lost, condemned, or dead? With a willing heart and a lifted veil, you will begin to see God's Word in a whole new way.

So with this truth in place, we can rest assured, knowing that our lives will be transformed upon our surrender to the truth, even if it begins with just accepting this challenge. And just know, God did not say that He would upcycle that which you already have and simply tweak a few things, nor did He say He would only transform part of your mind and heart. God has promised to give us a completely new heart and a mind that is just like Christ's.

And let us not forget, Jesus is the One who set us free and will continue to lead us into freedom. Jesus is the One who died on the cross so that we could die with Him, and Jesus is the One who was resurrected so we could have a new life. Jesus did declare that you are free now, in the moment when you believed in the Son. For the Word says, "Who the Son sets free is free indeed" (John 8:36 ESV).

(Note to self: This is a great verse for your tool box.)

And you are also set free when you choose to believe and surrender to Jesus Christ as your Lord and Saviour, as you allow the Holy Spirit to give you new life. How could your new life be like your old life, if you died and are a new creation in Jesus? You are free.

There is no arguing it, no recanting it, for you are free.

That's worth a huge shout-out, am I right? I know; Imma shoutin' it up right now. Well, perhaps you would if you thought it was meant for you personally, right? Just like I mentioned earlier on, God's love applies to others, but not to me (oh, not anymore, my dear friends). We must now press into this very truth and claim it as our own; we are free. Not others. Not those more qualified. "Who the Son sets free is free indeed." That's a truth you can shove in your tool box, my friends; if there is still room in there. Perhaps we need to visit the hardware store for a larger tool chest? Oh, you know I'm game (bigger is always better when it comes to power tools and the like).

Maybe you still don't see yourself as worthy of such amazing grace, love, hope, or freedom. My beloved, that type of song is not found on God's LMA record for you. It's in that place of believing lies and half-truths that the narrative of partial freedom closes the door on your mental prison that God has already freed you from.

God didn't create you anew in Jesus so that you would be gripped with anxiety, dark thoughts, or misunderstood beliefs. He did not give you a record player of a mind so you could listen to the devil's lies. He did not create you to be bound to the devil, to look like the devil, to fellowship with the devil, or to believe the devil. The devil did not create you, and the devil is not your Lord. The devil did not save you, and the devil did not free you. The devil entrapped you, stole you, controlled you, and consumed you.

But praise be to Jesus, who bore your slavery on His free shoulders and laid His life down on the cross so you could be resurrected from yours. Why would God create you to be in bondage to the devil when the devil came to steal, kill, and destroy?

When we look at how God describes the devil, it's quite clear that he is not our Lord, nor is he our intended plan. He is our adversary, our destroyer, our enemy. If he is your enemy, then how much more is he God's enemy? For he was God's enemy first, and he chose to revolt against God by targeting His children. Never once does the Bible declare over us that we are to be in bondage and held captive to the devil and his schemes. Never once has God promised us that our lives were to be enveloped by fear, darkness, and the control of sin. The Bible is very clear that we are not held by such things, but by the hands of God Himself.

We must understand fully that we have an enemy that only comes to steal, kill, and destroy. He comes to take away our hopes and dreams, to destroy that which our Father has purposed and ordered for us. The devil himself comes like a lion, seeking whom he may devour, but we have the Lord on our side, living within us through the power of the Holy Spirit.

And although the enemy is portrayed like a lion, let's remember that his roar is meaningless, harmless, and merely noisy at best.

For the Bible says we are overcomers with the power to overcome all the works of the devil, for Jesus has given us all authority over the devil and his schemes (Luke 10:19).

> For the devil comes only to steal, kill, and destroy, but our Lord Jesus has come so that we can have abundant life! (John 10:10 NIV)

Based on all of this truth I've been putting in place, a total of fifty-three verses in this book alone, Jesus is our Triumphant Victor who can set anyone free, and He has chosen to set you free.

I pray you understand that you are not the SKD record that's been playing in your mind. I pray you understand that you are not the SKD jersey that you once wore. I pray you no longer sit on the sidelines as though it were a noble place to exist, but that you would inherit the birthrights God has given you through Jesus Christ and willingly partake as the valuable team member God created you to be.

Let me pose an obvious question here: Do you know, believe, understand, and accept that you are free? Can you confidently say that through the Holy Spirit, you have the power to overcome the enemy, sin, and temptation? Do you know that you are a new creation, with a new nature, a new heart, and a new mind? Do you know that your life is meant to be lived abundantly? Do you know that you were created with and for a purpose? Do you know that you are loved with an everlasting love? That your identity is not in what you are, but to whom you belong?

I trust that you have been able to answer these questions, along with the others proposed in this book, and now can come away with a greater understanding of the life Jesus purchased for you with His blood.

I am confident that you will walk away with a desire to know Jesus more intimately and to solidify your understanding of the truth and freedom, while you seek to answer the above questions. So here is my final question:

Are you ready for this challenge?

Are you ready to fully embrace the incredible truths found in God's Word? Are you ready to walk in true freedom in Christ while you are still alive on this earth?

I trust that this book has not only challenged you but encouraged you to see who you truly are to God and in Christ Jesus. For the relationship that you were created for is rich, beautiful, exceptional, and abundant.

You are His beloved.

You are the bride of Christ.

You are free.

You are chosen.

You are brand new.

And you are absolutely beautiful in Him and to Him. (Quick, shove these last remaining tools in your toolbox. I never leave home without them.)

Final Thoughts

*Farewell for now, friends. If not here, I will
see you at the Father's house.*

Wow. I can't believe that we made it to the final chapter. The whole book-writing adventure complete. I must first and foremost give thanks to God for His unwavering guidance, help, and insight. All that I have learned and penned has been at His lead and direction. Second, I must give thanks to Julia for being such a huge support and competent writer alongside me. I had no idea how talented she was, nor how well our styles would fuse together. And last but by no means least, thank you to each of you for reading of my experiences, analogies, and Dawn-isms. I trust you've been able to see the dance of our words and thoughts. And even moreso, you've been able to see, read, and understand the freedom that we take such great delight in.

Can you recall back to chapter 1, where I disclosed my artistic expression of a tattoo, Beloved? I am proud to say that upon conclusion of this book, I am considering another. Just kidding. If I was actually going to consider one, though, it would be another simple one, an all-encompassing word for what I have learned during the writing of this book. Okay, chapter 1 was some time ago, so let me refresh your memory: Beloved. The new one would have to be another "B" word. Oh, for sure and for certain, I wouldn't disclose that here and now; I must at least keep you reading with suspense for at least another few paragraphs, right?

To be honest, these concluding thoughts have been more challenging than the writing of the whole book. I question the why and how comes, as I'm sure you are right now. How could just a simple sign-off and "Thanks a bunch" be hard to write, articulate, and pen?

Just now, I feel as though I have discovered, met, and fallen in love with a forever friend, and now I have to say goodbye in some way and let the friend move on to meet others and bless them as they have blessed me. I have come to see this book journey as a close and dear friend, dear to my heart. Tears even now fill my eyes as I begin the grieving process that I didn't know that I was about to face. Hanging on and yet letting go. I think I need a hanky. Oh, dear ones, my heart is so full for all that God has done in this process, all that He's done in and through me. I am humbled that I was chosen to write anything for that matter, but moreso, to pen such transformative and treasured truths. Given the privilege to showcase my beloved Jesus! Bringing honor and glory for all that He has done for us, His Bride.

I am incredibly excited to see what the Holy Spirit is going to do in and through you through His incredible power and through the scriptures. You are in for a change like none other. I promise you that my friend (this book) and, even moreso, my beloved Jesus is going to transform your heart, mind, and life. Hang onto your hats, dear ones. The winds of change have been blowing over you already, and I know that you are going to see Jesus more and more in the most incredible ways. Guaranteed.

So how do I see Jesus now? With an unveiled face. What does that look like? With the veil of lies and deception lifted, I now bow before Him with tears streaming down my cheeks. I am filled with gratitude and thanksgiving that cannot be uttered with human terms. In His eyes, there is the deepest of love and the most comforting compassion. There is peace beyond words. There is this incredible desire to embrace. To dance. To shout. The emotions run deep. For no longer am I hidden behind a veil. I behold my beloved,

Jesus. And do you see Him too? Are you crying along with me as you see Jesus, our beloved, through an unveiled face? Isn't this just incredible? Isn't He just incredible? Beholding your beloved. Let me just excuse myself here as I leave the two of you alone, beholding each other on your own journey to intimacy.

CPSIA information can be obtained
at www.ICGtesting.com
Printed in the USA
BVHW032324050521
606478BV00001B/17